Six Skills by Age Six

Six Skills by Age Six

Launching Early Literacy
at the Library

Anna Foote and Bradley Debrick

LIBRARIES
UNLIMITED™
An Imprint of ABC-CLIO, LLC
Santa Barbara, California • Denver, Colorado

Library of Congress Cataloging-in-Publication Data

Names: Foote, Anna, author. | Debrick, Bradley, author.
Title: Six skills by age six : launching early literacy at the library / Anna Foote and Bradley Debrick.
Description: Santa Barbara, CA : Libraries Unlimited, [2016] | Includes bibliographical references and index.
Identifiers: LCCN 2015031400| ISBN 9781610698993 (paperback) | ISBN 9781610699006 (ebook)
Subjects: LCSH: Children's libraries—Activity programs—United States. | Libraries and preschool children. | Libraries and caregivers. | Language arts (Preschool) | Reading readiness. | Storytelling. | Literacy programs—Kansas—Case studies. | BISAC: LANGUAGE ARTS & DISCIPLINES / Library & Information Science / General. | EDUCATION / Teaching Methods & Materials / Reading & Phonics.
Classification: LCC Z718.3 .F58 2016 | DDC 027.62/5—dc23 LC record available at http://lccn.loc.gov/2015031400

ISBN: 978-1-61069-899-3
EISBN: 978-1-61069-900-6

20 19 18 17 16   1 2 3 4 5

This book is also available on the World Wide Web as an eBook.
Visit www.abc-clio.com for details.

Libraries Unlimited
An Imprint of ABC-CLIO, LLC

ABC-CLIO, LLC
130 Cremona Drive, P.O. Box 1911
Santa Barbara, California 93116-1911

This book is printed on acid-free paper ∞

Manufactured in the United States of America

Illustrations created by Brad Sneed. Copyright © 2009 by Johnson County Library.

Contents

CHAPTER 8: LOOK FOR LETTERS EVERYWHERE 163

CHAPTER 9: TELL STORIES ABOUT EVERYTHING 189

Foreword

As one of the national trainers for library staff on the Every Child Ready to Read® initiative from the American Library Association, it is gratifying to see how Every Child Ready to Read® (ECRR) has been a catalyst for Johnson County (KS) Library and the State Library of Kansas's **6 by 6** initiative. As a children's librarian with Montgomery County (MD) Public Libraries when the county was a pilot site for ECRR, I, like the staff at Johnson County, came to realize the public library's role in helping children enter school ready to learn to read, and the necessity of reaching parents and caregivers to help accomplish this. ECRR gave us the foundation to acknowledge and build our early literacy initiative in intentional ways.

From a simple, modest beginning, **6 by 6** and this book show how far one can go with dedicated library staff who continually think and rethink ways to serve parents, caregivers, and families around early literacy. *Six Skills by Age Six: Launching Early Literacy at the Library* offers details in both process and content to help you envision your library's early literacy initiative, to create and develop one, or to build on what you already are doing. The areas covered are staff training, community outreach, parent workshops, storytimes, booklists, and children's activity kits.

As you proceed, remember that it is important to not just lift content from a model, but rather to use the process to develop what will become your library's own early literacy initiative that responds to your communities, resources, and goals. The authors have offered both philosophical approaches and practical advice to support your efforts. I hope you will be inspired as you use their knowledge and expertise, adding to your own, as you look for ways to raise the bar for informal education in your community, with the library as an advocate and key player to help all children enter school ready to learn.

Saroj Ghoting

Preface

The Beginning of an Early Literacy Initiative

Early literacy has always been important to public libraries, but in the new millennium, it has become even more core to library services, and formalized through ALA's Every Child Ready to Read® initiative.

After trial-and-error attempts with implementation, the staff at the Johnson County Library realized that every library had specialized materials and expert staff unlike any other business or agency. They subsequently adapted the standard Every Child Ready to Read® early literacy program (version 1) to suit needs of their library's communities and stakeholders. The result was a program called **6 by 6: Ready to Read,** which showcased the six skills kids should have experienced by their sixth birthday in order to become successful readers.

Kasey Laine Riley, former communications manager for Johnson County Library, describes the relationship of public libraries and early literacy education this way: "The public library plays a unique and special role in the community. The public library is uniquely equipped with staff who are truly committed to literacy for the good of the entire community. The development of an 'easy access' program such as **6 by 6** enables library staff to communicate a clear path to early literacy—and lifelong learning—through the six skills a child can develop by the age of six."

The program was so successful and popular that it caught the eye of the state librarian. In 2011, Joanne Budler, state librarian of Kansas, decided to adopt **6 by 6: Ready to Read** as the premier early literacy initiative for the state's public libraries. Recognizing the importance of early literacy to school and lifelong achievement, she approached Johnson County Library staff to request their permission and assistance in making the **6 by 6** program available to all Kansas public libraries.

Later that year, State Library staff convened a **6 by 6** launch committee composed of library staff members from across the state. These committee members were trained in **6 by 6** methodologies by Johnson County Library staff, and subsequently trained other library staff members at sessions held throughout the state.

To support the launch, the State Library used federal Institute of Museum and Library Services funds to print **6 by 6** informational materials for libraries to distribute to patrons. (Details about these materials can be found in Chapter 1.)

In 2012, State Library staff made a successful grant request to the Kansas Children's Cabinet and Trust Fund and was awarded $312,479 to support the implementation of **6 by 6** in Kansas libraries. The grant funded the following actions:

- the creation and circulation of early literacy activity kits to the state's public libraries
- an evaluation of how well **6 by 6** works in early childhood education settings conducted by the University of Kansas
- the hiring of the State Library's early childhood/lifelong learning coordinator (Anna Foote)

A second year of funding from the Children's Cabinet in the amount of $269,611 ensured that libraries' early literacy work continued and expanded.

(You'll find more details of the state's implementation of **6 by 6** in Chapter 1.)

Current Status of 6 by 6

The Johnson County Library heralded the sixth anniversary of **6 by 6** in 2015 with a multimonth celebration and a renewed focus on caregiver awareness. Activity spaces were enhanced at four neighborhood libraries, and special birthday artwork was featured heavily on the library's website and print materials. **6 by 6** has become a cornerstone of youth services at Johnson County Library.

Just before **6 by 6** reached this milestone, 80 percent of Kansas libraries reported that they were using the program in some way. Participation ranged, of course, from a stack of brochures on a checkout desk to an aggressive schedule of **6 by 6** storytimes and caregiver workshops, but the desired result is being achieved: Kansans have access to a high-quality, easily understandable way to prepare their children for a lifetime of reading.

We decided to write this book because of the tremendous professional satisfaction we have felt in tailoring an early literacy program to the needs of various communities in our state, starting with Johnson County, Kansas, and then expanding across the state to Kansas cities and towns of various sizes. We are eager to share with you our experiences and insight, not only into early literacy but into what it takes to make an early literacy program a deep and meaningful part of a community.

Combined, we have more than 30 years of work with children in library settings. Because Anna has worked with **6 by 6** at Johnson County Library and at the State Library, she has a deep knowledge of how **6 by 6** can work in libraries of various sizes and with families with differing levels of resources and education. She also shares her perspective on how libraries have tailored **6 by 6** to meet their unique communities' needs.

Bradley's tenure at Johnson County spans the concept, development, launch, and modifications that have made **6 by 6** what it is today. His experience in promoting early literacy to caregivers and community groups while keeping it fresh for patrons who visit the library means he is able to offer plenty of ideas about how you can make your library a key player in the early literacy development of children in your area.

Conclusion

With this book, you are invited to take a look at not only the development and first six years of **6 by 6** but also at the overall importance of early literacy to our communities. Consider the impact an early literacy program can have when you make it a deep and meaningful part of your community.

Reference

Riley, Kasey Laine, personal communication with the authors, March 2015.

Introduction:
The Importance of Early Literacy

Welcome

In this book, you're invited to take a closer look at early literacy and consider how developing a program that meets the unique needs of your community can benefit the children and adults who reside there. We'll provide you with details of our experiences in creating a unique early literacy program and then adapting it to communities of various sizes and situations across the state of Kansas with the hope that you can build on our experiences in your community.

The primary audience for this book is library staff, but other caregivers, including early childhood educators and family members of young children, can find the ideas presented here useful in their daily interactions with young children.

In chapters 1–3, you'll learn about the practicalities of starting an early literacy initiative, gaining staff and community support, and helping children learn the six skills necessary to be ready to learn to read at about age six.

Chapters 4–9 cover the six skills children need to have experienced by about age six to be ready to learn to read. One chapter is dedicated to each skill, and each chapter features activities and specific books that help enhance these skills in children. You'll also discover how each skill relates to the other five and how the skills link to lifelong learning. Each chapter concludes with a storytime for each of three age groups, along with a reproducible storytime plan for each group.

And finally, the book's conclusion discusses the usefulness of tailoring an early literacy initiative to individual communities.

Emergent versus Early Literacy

Nearly 50 years ago, Marie Clay, a researcher from New Zealand, introduced the term *emergent literacy*. Her definition focused on the early interactions children have with books and the knowledge about books and reading they gained from those interactions. The theory makes perfect sense: experiences yield proficiencies. The word *emergent*, however, gives us pause. It implies a hands-off approach. Literacy will happen naturally like a crocus emerging from cold soil. A different term—and one to which the authors of this book subscribe—is *early literacy*.

The definition of early literacy is "what children know about reading and writing before they can actually read and write" (Every Child Ready to Read® Manual). This definition takes a wide approach to literacy development and amplifies the caregivers' role in the process. Every Child Ready to Read® introduced public libraries to six pre-reading concepts (we call them skills) and also gave library staff tips on engaging caregivers with the literacy development of their children. We will discuss these skills further in Chapter 1, and chapters 4–9 are dedicated to a full exploration of each of these six skills.

What Is 6 by 6: Ready to Read?

6 by 6: Ready to Read is an early literacy program developed by the Johnson County (KS) Library. Based on the nationally released program Every Child Ready To Read®, **6 by 6: Ready to Read** identifies six pre-reading skills that all children should have experienced by their sixth birthday: six skills by six years. **6 by 6** involves more than just being aware of these skills, however. Children need to have many and varied interactions with these skills, and adults need to intentionally provide these experiences.

A robust early literacy package has been developed by the Johnson County Library that includes storytimes, booklists, children's activity kits, parent and caregiver workshops, librarian training, and community outreach. This book discusses the development of **6 by 6** and its implementation across Kansas.

Universal Skills

The six pre-reading skills established by Every Child Ready to Read® and adapted by Johnson County Library can be applied to any early childhood program or curriculum, including yours. It is not the mission of **6 by 6** to teach reading. Instead, **6 by 6** seeks to help caregivers and childcare professionals build foundational skills so that children have an easier time learning to read under any pedagogy and in any educational environment.

Being a library-based program, it uses children's books as a primary tool. However, there are ways to support and develop pre-reading skills in all environments. One goal of **6 by 6** is to get caregivers thinking about early literacy not just at the library but everywhere—grocery store, stoplight, or playground.

Families for whom English is not the primary language are encouraged to practice the skills in their native language so children hear the rhythms of speech. **6 by 6 en Español** is being developed more fully in Johnson County so that the library can effectively reach the growing number of Latino parents and impart the important role they play in the early literacy development of their children.

Looking Ahead

In Chapter 1, the transition from Every Child Ready to Read® to **6 by 6** and the principles that guided our work are detailed. We'll also further explore the adoption and expansion of **6 by 6** by the State Library of Kansas.

Reference

Every Child Ready to Read @ Your Library Training Kit. 1st ed. Chicago, IL: Public Library Association; Association for Library Service to Children, 2004.

Chapter 1

From National to Local:
A Brief History of **6 by 6**

Every Child Ready to Read®

When the National Reading Panel (a group convened by the National Institute of Child Health and Human Development) released their report "Teaching Children to Read" in 2000, the NICHD formed a partnership with the Public Library Association to develop a program that would "enlist parents and caregivers as partners in preparing their children for learning to read and to provide the most effective methods to achieve this end." The Public Library Association joined with the Association for Library Service to Children to test the program and package it for use in public libraries throughout the country.

After two years of trials and evaluations, the first edition of Every Child Ready to Read® was released in 2004 and described by ALSC as a parent education initiative that stressed the primary caregiver's role as a child's first teacher and role model. Every Child Ready to Read® featured six pre-reading skills, each of which is explained more thoroughly in later chapters:

- Print Motivation
- Vocabulary
- Phonological Awareness
- Print Awareness
- Letter Knowledge
- Narrative Skills

The program also unveiled three distinct age-group categories that helped caregivers identify benchmarks and milestones for the children in their care:

- **Early Talkers**—birth to approximately 18 months
- **Talkers**—approximately 18 months to three years
- **Pre-Readers**—approximately ages three to five years

Every Child Ready to Read® was packaged and sold to public libraries with an instruction manual, timed presentations, demonstration manipulatives and books, brochures, posters, research handouts, booklists, and access to an extensive website. In addition to the printed materials, a corps of approved Every Child Ready to Read® trainers traversed the country providing workshops and how-to demonstrations for public library staff.

Johnson County Library was an early adopter of Every Child Ready to Read® and relied upon the program extensively in storytimes and outreach for three years. All youth services staff attended two full days of training that showed them how to intentionally incorporate the skills into storytime and how to converse with caregivers to maximize their library time. After the training, a small cadre led by Youth Outreach Librarian Kathy McLellan began making early literacy presentations in the community. Every Child Ready to Read® was incorporated into storytimes, and flyers were made available to the general public and sent directly to childcare centers.

Transitioning from Every Child Ready to Read® to 6 by 6

Even with all of these wonderful resources, a 2010 evaluation of Every Child Ready to Read® (ECRR) by academic researchers Susan B. Neuman and Donna Celano showed many librarians felt the program was intimidating, costly, not critical to their mission, and/or in conflict with other previously established early literacy programs. Eventually, for some of those same reasons, use of the program began to wane at Johnson County Library, and a small group of library staffers began to retool Every Child Ready to Read® into a new program, **6 by 6**.

As much as we liked and used the first edition of Every Child Ready to Read®, we recognized that it was aimed at library staff and that some of the language (terms like Phonological Awareness) could be off-putting to parents and others who were not familiar with early childhood education. Our team set out to create an early literacy program that was directed toward the families, the childcare providers, and the early childhood educators we serve. We wanted an attractive program with straightforward language that would emphasize how adults can use everyday interactions with children to get them ready to learn to read.

With this in mind, we chose to make simplified language and child-friendly art the hallmarks of our program. We wanted to create a brand that would be instantly recognizable and associated with the library. We chose to name our program **6 by 6: Ready to Read**, highlighting the six skills every child needs to have experienced by about age six to be ready to learn to read.

The reinvention was initially led by Kasey Laine Riley, former communications manager the Johnson County Library. In e-mail communication with the authors, Riley stated, "The public library plays a unique and special role in the community. The public library is uniquely equipped with staff who are truly committed to literacy for the good of the entire community. The development of an 'easy access' program such as **6 by 6** enables library staff to communicate a clear path to early literacy." Easy access was paramount, so one of the first issues at hand was renaming the skills.

Simplified Language

In making the transition from Every Child Ready to Read® to **6 by 6: Ready to Read**, the Johnson County Library retained the three age-group categories and names, but changed the skill phrases as follows:

- Print Motivation became **Have Fun With Books**
- Vocabulary became **Talk Talk Talk**
- Phonological Awareness became **Take Time to Rhyme, Sing and Play Word Games**
- Print Awareness became **Notice Print All Around You**
- Letter Knowledge became **Look for Letters Everywhere**
- Narrative Skills became **Tell Stories About Everything**

Decoding and Comprehension

Regardless of the phrasing, the six pre-reading skills can be further divided into two categories: skills that help children learn to read (decoding) and skills that help children read to learn (comprehension).

Decoding, at its very heart, is taking figures or symbols you cannot understand and converting them into something you can. An example in context would be the process of seeing a squiggly line on a page, recognizing that squiggly line is the letter /s/, recalling the sound of the letter /s/, repeating the process with adjacent squiggly lines, and finally blending all of the sounds to form a word.

The three decoding skills, in **6 by 6** terms, are **Look for Letters**, **Take Time to Rhyme**, and **Notice Print**. Once children have mastered those skills, they will not need to revisit them again. There are no more letters to learn (unless, of course, the child studies a foreign language), the child knows and can aurally identify all of the 44 phonemes made with our alphabet, and the child is aware of print and its importance in his or her life. Those skills are finite, and mastery equals completion.

Comprehension is a different matter. The three comprehension skills are **Talk Talk Talk**, **Tell Stories About Everything**, and **Have Fun With Books**. These skills begin at birth and last a lifetime. Even as adults, we should continue to appreciate and augment our comprehension skills. These are abilities that bring joy to reading and allow us to communicate effectively. Children (and adults) should constantly strive to learn new vocabulary, seek out a good story, and enjoy the experience of reading.

Child-Friendly Art

A second key step to converting Every Child Ready to Read® to **6 by 6** was the development of images for the program that would be engaging to children and adults. Johnson County Library is fortunate to have a good friend in Brad Sneed, a well-known children's book author and illustrator. Sneed created six charming animal characters, one for each of the skills.

The characters are printed in full color on the cover of this book. Sneed customized each of the six characters to represent one of the six skills:

- A playful Monkey represents **Have Fun With Books**.
- A T-shaped Toucan represents **Talk Talk Talk**.
- A Goat in a coat eating oats on a boat represents **Take Time to Rhyme, Sing and Play Word Games**.
- A Kangaroo with her map-reading Joey represents **Notice Print All Around You**.
- An unusual and alphabetic Peacock represents **Look for Letters Everywhere**.
- A book-focused Turtle represents **Tell Stories About Everything**.

These attractive images have served our goal of engaging the community very well—they are distinctive, attractive, and associated with the library. They have also given us an unanticipated bonus: library staff members find them helpful in remembering and recognizing the skills when they are creating activities and designing training sessions.

The Johnson County Library sought and received permission from the Association for Library Service to Children to make these changes and to develop a separate—yet strongly parallel—local early literacy program based on the 2004 version of Every Child Ready to Read®. All due credit is given to the National Institute of Child Health and Human Development, the Public Library Association, and the Association for Library Service to Children. A second version of Every Child Ready to Read® was released by PLA and ALSC in 2011.

Ages and Stages

As mentioned earlier, **6 by 6** retained the same age-group categories from Every Child Ready to Read®:

- **Early Talkers**— birth to approximately 18 months

- **Talkers**—approximately 18 months to three years
- **Pre-Readers**—approximately ages three to five years

You likely noticed the overlap between **Talker** and **Pre-Reader**. Since brain development is rapid in the first five years, there is an overlap to accommodate individual rates of development. These age groups serve several purposes. First, they help caregivers relate **6 by 6** to the ages and abilities of the children in their care. Second, the age groups begin at birth, which shows that the library values early literacy for the very young and that it welcomes babies and is ready to assist with their needs. Third, the age groups guide library staff in planning storytimes and activities. The age groups are very important when planning storytimes, but less important when planning play activities. Children naturally play in their own way and at the developmental level appropriate for them. Foam blocks for a two-year-old are just as effective as foam blocks for a six-year-old even though they play with them in very different ways. As long as the toys and manipulatives are safe, they can be used with all three age groups.

We provide storytime plans for the three age groups in chapters 4–9.

The Birthplace of 6 by 6: Johnson County, Kansas

The Johnson County Library is a 13-building library system that serves the southwest quadrant of the Kansas City metropolitan area. Within the county borders are six school districts, 20 municipalities, and an estimated population of 570,000. Approximately 40,000 residents are children under five.

At start-up in 2009, the day-to-day costs of **6 by 6** were paid from a general library budget line item administered by the youth outreach librarian. This budget was used primarily to pay for materials for the first early literacy activity space, initial training for the youth services staff, and supplies for caregiver workshops. Funding for program materials, including those used for promotion, was paid via the communications manager. The initial costs for those components were paid using some grant monies received from the Kansas Health Foundation and from a Kansas-based savings-and-loan institution.

The Johnson County Library Foundation also secured funds to purchase an interactive early literacy station designed and fabricated by the Burgeon Group of Phoenix, Arizona. The initial year was the largest investment of funds, with smaller, as-needed purchases made subsequently.

In 2012, the performance expectations of the youth outreach librarian were changed along with the position title. The new position, early literacy coordinating librarian, was to oversee all aspects of **6 by 6**, including assisting with grant administration. The new position has a narrower scope but a deeper involvement in early literacy.

The State Library Adopts and Expands 6 by 6
Timeline

In 2011, Joanne Budler, state librarian of Kansas, decided to adopt **6 by 6: Ready to Read** as the state's early literacy initiative for public libraries. She recognized the role early literacy plays in creating a foundation for lifelong success. She approached Johnson County Library staff for their permission and assistance in making **6 by 6** available to all Kansas public libraries.

Later that year, State Library staff convened a **6 by 6** launch committee, whose members were trained in **6 by 6** by Johnson County Library staff. Committee members subsequently trained other library staff members at sessions held throughout the state.

The State Library printed **6 by 6** informational materials for libraries to display and to distribute to patrons. More details about these materials can be found below.

In 2012, the State Library received a grant from the Kansas Children's Cabinet and Trust Fund and was awarded $312,479 to support the implementation of **6 by 6** in Kansas libraries. The grant funded the following actions:

- The creation and circulation of early literacy activity kits to the state's public libraries.
- An evaluation of how well **6 by 6** works in early childhood education settings conducted by the University of Kansas.
- The hiring of the State Library's early childhood/lifelong learning coordinator (Anna Foote).

A second year of funding from the Children's Cabinet in the amount of $269,611 ensured that libraries' early literacy work continued and expanded.

Informational Materials

High-quality, attractive informational materials have been crucial to creating community awareness of **6 by 6** as the local library's early literacy program. Johnson County Library and State Library staff have arranged for the printing of these materials, and have distributed them to local public libraries, with assistance from Kansas Regional Library System staff. Local libraries use the materials to draw attention to their early literacy initiatives. Library staff also use the materials to educate community members about the importance of early literacy and how to foster it in children.

To date, the State Library has made the following informational pieces available to participating libraries:

- Posters
- Trifold brochures (in English and in Spanish)
- Card sets (in English and in Spanish)
- Magnet sheets (bilingual)

Examples of posters, brochures, and card sets may be seen on the State Library's website: kslib.info/6by6.

The magnets are a later piece made available to Kansas librarians in 2014. We designed a perforated sheet of magnets that can be separated into six separate magnets, one for each skill. The design is very simple, with each magnet featuring a large image of one of the **6 by 6** characters along with the skill name in English and in Spanish, and the state's **6 by 6** web address. The magnets have proven very attractive and popular with families throughout the state.

Staff Training

As mentioned earlier, training library staff has been key to implementation of **6 by 6** in the state. Training began with a "train the trainers" event at Johnson County Library, Antioch, in 2011. Those trainers then presented training sessions for librarians and child caregivers (including parents) at locations throughout the state. **6 by 6** training for library staff and child caregivers is ongoing and is being conducted by state, regional, and local library staff, in addition to those trainers from the initial group. We address the content of the training sessions in more detail in Chapter 2.

Most library staff members who serve children have at least a basic knowledge of early literacy concepts and techniques. However, librarians have not traditionally thought of themselves as experts in the field, nor have they considered their role as one of educating adults about early literacy.

In fact, for **6 by 6** to succeed, library staff needed to embrace both of these thoughts. So our training focused on intentionality—giving library staffers the understanding that the public does view librarians as experts in early literacy, and helping staff know that people who care for children want expert early literacy advice. In our training sessions, we focused on giving staff practical, straightforward phrases that they could use with adults, whether as a literacy aside given to adults during storytime, or during conversations while families are exploring an early literacy activity in the library. We impress upon library staff that demonstrating early literacy behaviors for adults is important—but equally important is taking a moment to explain to those adults why you are doing what you are doing.

Melendra Sutliff Sanders, children's consultant at North Central Kansas Libraries System, is responsible for providing **6 by 6** training for library staff in her region. Via an e-mail to the authors, she advised people new to **6 by 6** that they should "get comfortable explaining what early literacy is and how the activities the library encourages enhance early literacy skills. Don't make your advice so generic that caregivers assume they are already doing the things you're promoting. Many parents do some of the things, many parents do none of the things. As experts in early literacy practice, librarians need to be comfortable teaching parents the best ways to help their children. This means librarians need to do a lot of demonstrating (whether in storytime or during in-library activities)."

Outreach

As with Every Child Ready to Read®, **6 by 6** emphasizes the importance of outreach in making a community's early literacy program a success. Every child in the community needs to experience early literacy skills to be ready to learn to read, which means it's important for library staff to carry the message—and the method—into the community.

With this in mind, State Library staff chose to emphasize outreach in two ways as we began to implement **6 by 6**. We contracted with the University of Kansas to perform an independent evaluation of how well **6 by 6** works in childcare programs, and we developed a simple outreach method called Checkup and Check Out. Details on both of these can be found in Chapter 2.

Looking Ahead

Now that you've learned about the transition from Every Child Ready to Read® to **6 by 6** and the program's expansion throughout Kansas, turn to Chapter 2, where you'll explore the nuts and bolts of establishing an early literacy program in your state.

References

"Report of the National Reading Panel: Teaching Children to Read." National Reading Panel Publications. April 1, 2000. http://www.nichd.nih.gov/publications/pubs/nrp/documents/report.pdf. Accessed March 31, 2015.

Riley, Kasey Laine, personal communication with the authors, March 2015.

Sanders, Melendra Sutliff, personal communication with the authors, March 2015.

Chapter 2

Establishing an Early Literacy Program

Assessing Community Needs

Many libraries include a needs assessment as part of a strategic plan or master plan. It's possible to get a broad sense of your community's needs by doing some basic demographics research. The U.S. Census Bureau can provide you with an estimate of the number of residents under five years old, education level of adults, and a basic idea of the languages your library patrons speak at home. A good place to start is at the Bureau's website: http://www.census.gov/.

The census, however, is conducted only every ten years, so keep in mind that the information may be out of date, especially if your community has experienced a major economic loss or gain that impacted the population. If your library is an agency of a local government, you may be able to use interagency connections and gain access to a larger pool of data that can help identify the needs of your patrons.

For example, at the beginning, the Johnson County Library chose to focus **6 by 6** on "at-risk" families and childcare centers. That term, however, is subjective. A child from a low-income family is no more "at risk" than a child from an affluent family whose parent is glued to his or her electronic devices. But any initiative must begin with some scope of service, and **6 by 6** started as a way to reach at-risk children. The library relied on information from local health departments and childcare provider networks to determine the areas of the county that best fit this designation, initially targeting childcare programs in lower-income areas and English-language-learning families.

You might start with the same criteria, or perhaps you want to look at the education level of the families or childcare providers in a certain area. At some childcare centers, frequent turnover rate of staff is a concern because it can indicate that staff members may not be equipped to provide high-quality experiences for children, whether due to lack of experience, lack of education, or both.

If analyzing census data seems daunting, begin with a program where participating families are already vetted as being "at risk." For example, Women, Infants, and Children (WIC) participants and Head Start families must meet low-income requirements. Working with organizations like these can also factor into your outreach efforts. More on that later in the chapter.

Obtaining Staff Support

Launching a major initiative like **6 by 6** requires buy-in from a number of participants. (Of course, the players and process may look very different at different libraries.) At our library, the communications manager, youth outreach librarian, and youth services manager sketched out the idea, and it was presented to the county librarian who, according to Kasey Laine Riley, former communications manager, "immediately recognized the value of a well-packaged, visually appealing early childhood literacy program."

Including **6 by 6** in the library's strategic plan, which was under development at the time, encouraged all departments to think about early literacy and how they could (and would) be involved in making this idea a cornerstone of library service.

If you are unable to incorporate your early literacy initiative into your library's strategic plan, be sure to get approval and support from as many managers, administrators, board members, and Friends as possible. Explain to them how an early literacy initiative benefits the entire community and can be a flagship program for your library. Even informal support for your initiative will go a long way in ensuring its success.

Administrators and Board Members

Backing by administration and trustees demonstrates commitment to the program. Administrators and board members can serve as your program's public face, as they did with **6 by 6** in Johnson County, and can be relied upon to answer questions from staff and media as well as lobby for budgetary support. Enlist building managers to think about **6 by 6** when scheduling staff. Additional time may be needed for programming, outreach, and cleaning of the early literacy activity space (more on that below).

Front-Line Staff

To keep your early literacy message clear and consistent, be sure to train everyone who engages with the public. With **6 by 6**, the youth services manager and the youth outreach librarian conducted workshops for all library staff members. Conducting small-group sessions will give you plenty of time for questions and to address location-specific issues. Information provided during these workshops can help staff develop phrases and approaches for working with caregivers of young children.

One major concern of youth service staff is how to talk to caregivers without coming across as judgmental or patronizing. An open discussion of these concerns along with role-play during these staff presentations can alleviate some of these fears. The training can also include a refresher on children's book categories (picture, reader, chapter, and the like) so that, at a minimum, everyone who had contact with patrons in the stacks will be able to confidently direct them to the most appropriate section.

Early Literacy Cadre

Our youth services manager created a team of 10 early literacy specialists called the **6 by 6** Cadre. Whatever terminology you use, you should have a group that can serve as the go-to coworkers, who can better explain early literacy and ensure its place in the library buildings. These staff members can also maintain online booklists for each of the skills, answer questions submitted by patrons via the library's early literacy webpage, assist with the development of circulating theme kits, and help create in-branch programming and activities that support your early literacy endeavor.

If you are a one-person show, a cadre of staff members may not be feasible. But think broadly. Are there community members or agencies you can recruit to be part of your team? This is an excellent opportunity to call upon your community connections or forge new ones.

Facilities Team

The role of the facilities and maintenance team is easily overlooked, but its importance cannot be overstated. There are some special considerations for an early literacy initiative that can be addressed only by staff with facilities and maintenance experience. First, you may need to move furnishings to create activity spaces or a comfortable programming space.

Second, those spaces need a bit of special attention to maintain a level of safety appropriate for young children. A bit of peeling paint or chipped drywall in an adult area may not be a big deal, but the same issues in a space designed for babies could be hazardous. At Johnson County Library, general cleaning of the space was split between the building custodian and the youth services staff. The custodian was asked to clean and sanitize (to the best level possible) all of the tabletop surfaces and chairs and to vacuum the children's play spaces daily; youth staff were responsible for cleaning manipulatives used in the activity spaces. If possible, work with your local department of health and environment to develop cleaning protocols.

Adapting Your Collection

In preparing for the implementation of your early literacy program, it's a good idea to create or expand circulating themed book kits. Our kits, originally called Books To Grow, won an innovation award when created in the late 1990s, and they were marketed solely to childcare providers. During the system-wide rollout of **6 by 6**, we converted the kits—nearly 200 in total—to **6 by 6** Books To Go and made them available for regular checkout to all patrons. If you already have themed book kits that circulate, consider recycling and rebranding them for your early literacy initiative. If you don't have them, consider creating such a collection. Your collection development staff members can help with selecting new books and working with in-house and outsourced processing teams to prepare the refurbished kits.

Improving Web Content

If you can, tap into a web content developer or team to help build a brand new web page just for early literacy. This page can provide a simple overview of your program and serve as a repository for in-depth information about the skills and the age groups. It can also be the home of the early literacy booklists you create. Shortly after the launch of **6 by 6**, our web content team undertook an ambitious project to record and post live-action rhyme-demonstration videos. More than 90 videos were recorded, edited, and made available on the website. The web content team also managed a small grant that allowed the library to create DVDs of these action rhymes (also known as fingerplays), which were distributed to the public at all library locations. Consider ways in which you might further enhance your web presence to accommodate your early literacy efforts. Perhaps it's just a set of links to some outside resources, a set of YouTube recordings, or maybe you can create some content on your own.

Using Marketing and Communication to Promote Your Message

The most visible components of your efforts come from your marketing and communications efforts. This can be in the form of publicity and outreach as well as internal documents and support materials.

At our library, the marketing team developed attractive print materials that served a variety of functions from basic awareness (posters) to integral instructional pieces (card sets). When **6 by 6** was adopted by the State Library of Kansas, it was the marketing and communication team that assisted most with the transition, providing graphics files and best practices to make the transition a smooth one.

In a more traditional role, your marketing team might develop a press kit or coordinate a multimedia promotion of your program. Kasey Laine Riley states, "We utilized local newspaper, radio and television and enlisted a local TV station as a partner in the goal of early childhood literacy. We launched with a series of print ads accompanied by a television campaign that had the look and feel of a public service announcement rather than a TV ad. Early childhood literacy is as much of an appealing goal to local media as it is to libraries and such partnerships can be extremely effective in reaching large numbers of people in addition to lending credence to the program."

Obtaining Community Support

Once the library develops a presentation to serve as the cornerstone of outreach to childcare providers, you may wish to apply for approval of the curriculum by your state's department of education or department of health and environment. This will allow you to offer workshops to childcare providers at no cost to them, with the benefit of contact (or continuing education) hours toward their required certifications. Johnson County Library offers these presentations independently as well as in conjunction with other organizations such as the Johnson County Department of Health and Environment, the Mid-America Association for the Education of Young Children, and Johnson County Community College.

"Being involved with these groups gave us credibility and visibility," said former youth outreach librarian Kathy McLellan in an interview with one of the authors.

In addition, the childcare licensing office of your local department of education or health and environment might provide mailing labels that your library can use to reach licensed providers. In our case, the labels were provided for specific postal ZIP codes so our messages could be sent to the providers we determined served our target audience.

In addition to forming the partnerships mentioned above, reach out to local hospitals, Head Start programs, Parents as Teachers, and local universities and community colleges. This will help spread your message to a wider audience than you could ever reach independently. Look for ways to develop these relationships into full partnerships to benefit both parties. These benefits might include joint programming, shared meeting space, materials distribution, guest speakers, workshops, and letters of support.

For example, through an official memorandum of understanding, Johnson County Library provides an embedded librarian to Growing Futures Early Education Center, one of the largest Head Start affiliations in Johnson County. This librarian is on site one full day each month and provides readers' advisory and reference services to the center's staff, creates on-demand booklists for classroom use, serves as their building librarian, and provides storytimes to all of their pre-K classrooms. In exchange, Growing Futures provides the library with a place in their office to distribute **6 by 6** materials, helps promote Summer Reading, provides space for library programs, and allows the library to assist on open enrollment days by talking to new families about public library services.

Now that you've considered ways to develop and launch your new early literacy program, take a look at how these steps might look in your community.

Gathering the Necessary Resources

As you look to adapt or create an early literacy program for your community, think broadly about potential partners and supporters. An effective and strong early literacy initiative benefits the entire community, so be sure to consider every person, business, and agency as a potential supporter.

You might find these types of people and entities helpful:

- Graphic designers
- Artists/illustrators
- Copywriters
- Print shops
- Crafters/craft stores
- Marketing/public relations firms
- Media outlets
- Various child- and family-serving agencies (as noted above)

Establishing (or expanding) a strong relationship with local media outlets can be doubly beneficial. Promoting your program will allow you to reach more of the people you want to serve, plus it will alert potential supporters to the good work you are doing and the needs of your library.

At Johnson County Library, getting media coverage for **6 by 6** went smoothly. As noted, former communications manager Kasey Laine Riley found early childhood literacy to be an appealing lure to local media. The message that the entire community benefits when children head to school ready to learn to read was one that local media found easy to represent in print and video. It gave media members an attractive, feel-good story about how libraries can benefit the community's youngest citizens and their families. Photographs and videos of groups of children enthusiastically enjoying early literacy activities and storytimes helped illustrate the stories and pull in readers and viewers.

If you encounter difficulty in getting media coverage, try one or more of the following methods.

Send out media releases. The most effective of these will be tailored to the specific media outlet—for example, releases you send to a radio station should read like a brief radio story, and ones you send to the newspaper should resemble a news article.

Distribute media packets, including any informational and promotional materials for your initiative, especially if they are high quality and would make good photographs or video illustrations.

In all your media communications, be sure to emphasize that your program has been created specifically for *your* community and is aimed at meeting its exact needs. Offer specific times when reporters and photographers would be most likely to encounter families enjoying your library's early literacy activities. (For example, before, during, and after regularly scheduled storytimes, or any time your library is typically busy with young families.)

If you have a relationship with any local media members, now is the time to use it! Be sure to check with other staff members, board members, and Friends to see if they have media contacts they can call upon.

Finding Funding

As with potential partners, cast a wide net when seeking possible funders. Consider approaching the following types of organizations:

- Local community foundations (these have been especially generous to several Kansas libraries)
- Service organizations—include school and college student organizations
- Local, state, and national grant-making agencies
- Businesses and organizations that can provide discounts, make in-kind donations, or assist with fundraising events

When approaching businesses and organizations, be clear about what you want and what you can offer, but also be ready to be flexible. For example, you may start by asking your local grocery store for a donation of deli meals for your family-night open house and end up paying a bit by agreeing to purchase the meals at the store's cost. For that type of donation, you may be willing to list the grocery store as a program sponsor on the materials promoting the open house.

Or the more exciting may happen—you approach the grocery store manager for a donation of meals, and she decides to make a substantial contribution of money to support your early literacy initiative. In this case, you may choose to put the store name and logo on all of the informational materials you print using those funds. (These will have a longer presence in the community and present a longer-lasting benefit to the store.)

Extending Outreach and Hosting Special Events

From the beginning, outreach has been a main component of **6 by 6**. Of course, in the public library, the time and staff available for outreach varies widely throughout the year. In a multibranch system, the perfect scenario would be to have the local branch library staff visit the centers and providers in their service area. In smaller communities, it might mean the librarian simply walking across the street!

No matter the situation, making that neighborhood connection can quickly develop into a relationship between the library and the childcare center that greatly benefits enrolled families. Besides, what librarian doesn't love being enthusiastically greeted by a doting preschooler who visits the library after school or on the weekend?

Plan your launch carefully and completely. When **6 by 6** launched in September 2009, a full week of activities was planned for different audiences. We offered a number of choices:

- Storytimes
- Storytellers
- Musicians
- Art workshops led by Brad Sneed, the **6 by 6** illustrator
- Early literacy workshops for parents
- Early literacy workshops for childcare providers
- Ribbon cutting with local dignitaries followed by library open house
- Kindergarten readiness screenings (vision, hearing, gross motor)
- Media interviews

You may or may not be able to offer something this extensive, but use your connections and your budget to make as big a splash as you can. Perhaps your library foundation or Friends group will provide funds to develop or enhance the activity space at your library. This investment can be celebrated with special programs and a ribbon cutting.

And don't forget to celebrate your successes along the way! For the sixth anniversary of **6 by 6**, author and illustrator Brad Sneed created new birthday-themed **6 by 6** animal characters, which were featured on the library's early literacy webpage and in all print materials used to promote the celebration.

Illustrator Brad Sneed created birthday animals to help celebrate the sixth anniversary of **6 by 6**.

Outreach Storytime

Second only to lending books, storytime is perhaps the most ubiquitous element of public library service. Attendance ebbs and flows for a number of reasons, but storytime remains one of the best ways to develop print motivation in children and demonstrate early literacy practices to adults.

Librarians are often asked to visit childcare programs to provide storytimes, an excellent way to reach children who may not be able to visit the library. Providing outreach storytime sessions is a balancing act, however. If you offer this service, you will undoubtedly have more teachers who would like storytime than you have hours available to visit. If a weekly visit is impossible, consider a quarterly or seasonal visit. If that is still too much of a stretch, set up a semiannual visit to coincide with Week of the Young Child or Library Card Sign-Up month.

Even though parents may not be attending these childcare center storytimes, you do have a unique opportunity to showcase early literacy skills to the providers at those locations. Be sure to ask staff to stay in the room during storytime to observe and participate. If they do not do this, make it a condition of your visit. Childcare workers are a very important audience for your early literacy message. Think of the number of children a childcare provider educates and influences over the course of a career!

Once you have made a connection with a childcare center, ask about parents' nights or open house events. Offer to provide flyers or activity calendars to their families, or, better yet, offer to set up a table where you can answer questions and encourage library card sign-up.

Another option is to host a storytime program at your library for the families of that childcare center, or even for families on its waiting list. An invitation specifically mentioning the childcare program's name may bring in some first-time visitors and give you a chance to make an excellent first impression and highlight all that your library has to offer.

Community Events

If your community has an annual fair or a weekly farmer's market, consider those locations as places for early literacy outreach. Meeting patrons (even nonpatrons!) in unexpected locations can have a big impact on their opinion of the library. In noisy and busy environments, holding storytime sessions may not be practical, but a table with library information or a few simple children's activities may be perfect. Johnson County Library regularly participates at movie nights coordinated by the local recreation district, Touch-a-Truck events, parades, and festivals. Booths at these events are generally free for nonprofit libraries, so your only significant investment would be time.

Community Book Displays

A passive but effective type of early literacy outreach is through community book displays. Johnson County Library maintains **6 by 6** book displays in two Women, Infants, and Children offices, two public health clinics, and one hospital maternity center. Most of these places already had book display units, but did not have a plan or the time to maintain them. The library offered to curate these displays by filling them with donated books or items deselected from the collection. An adhesive bookplate is positioned inside each book naming the library as the donor. You can also add flyers to the display or a small placard inviting readers to take books home.

Parent and Provider Workshops

The original Every Child Ready to Read® materials provided thorough presentation scripts that were used to instruct adults about early literacy. Johnson County Library used those presentations for a few years, tailored slightly to add the library logo and presenters' names. However, when **6 by 6** launched in 2009, the presentation was given a more extensive edit to include more library-specific information, photographs, and local statistics. Again, the research remains the same from Every Child Ready to Read®, but it has been repackaged to be easier for families to understand. We found this reformatting to be very effective with our adult audiences of child educators and family members.

Workshops for parents, who are not seeking contact hour credit for childcare licensing, should be 60 to 75 minutes long and should include the following topics:

- Welcome and introduction of presenter
- Research and brain development
- Early literacy skills with book examples and demonstrations
- Library overview
- Question and answer time

Our workshop that is approved for contact hour credits and generally presented to childcare professionals is a full two-hour workshop. This provider workshop includes the following topics:

- Welcome and introduction of presenter
- Introduction of participants (for small groups only)
- ECRR information
- Research and brain development
- Library services to childcare providers
- Group discussion of early literacy keywords
- Early literacy skills with research, book examples, and demonstrations
- Group discussion of classroom activity ideas that support literacy development
- Question and answer time
- Participants' evaluation of the session

If you have a high level of support and commitment from library staff, you might be able to provide a robust annual slate of training for family members and for child educators. If you are more of a one-person show, this likely won't be possible.

However, you can build your efforts slowly by recruiting highly qualified, dedicated volunteers to your growing cadre, who will help offer training sessions on behalf of your library. Volunteers of this type must be carefully screened and willing to make an ongoing commitment. You need people with an understanding of early literacy and child development, along with great presentation skills (or the ability to develop them). Initially, finding, screening, and training the right volunteers can take up a good deal of time, but as you build a corps of trained volunteers, they can help you find, orient, and train additional volunteers. Enthusiasm about serving young children and their caring adults is contagious!

State Library Implementation

Often, library staff understand that many of the families who use public library services and programs to benefit their young children already know the importance of early literacy and that they are already doing many daily activities to foster early literacy skills.

The issue then becomes one of outreach, bringing the early literacy message to those who aren't currently using library resources. Recognizing that **6 by 6** is for the whole community, State Library staff made the decision to help libraries focus on **6 by 6** outreach in two ways. First, University of Kansas researchers would study the effectiveness of **6 by 6** in childcare settings, using a visiting librarian model. Second, the State Library partnered with the Kansas Pediatric Foundation to establish a joint project, Checkup and Check Out: For Kansas Kids, detailed below.

Emphasizing outreach at a time when library staff and budgets are stretched thin is not easy, but considering how beneficial outreach was to Kansas communities, we encourage you to extend the benefits of your program to other communities across your state. What we found with our state study and new program surprised us—not only is outreach beneficial, but it can also be accomplished using a minimal amount of staff time.

Evaluating Your Early Literacy Initiative

Research is crucial in justifying funding your project. Consider including funding for an independent, rigorous evaluation of your program when you apply for grants or ask for funding. If this is impossible, collect patron surveys and anecdotes to help you make a case for continuing and building your early literacy program.

Implications for Outreach

As noted above, **6 by 6** researchers found that having library staff give childcare providers a brief early literacy training session and some simple handouts

In 2012, after our grant request was approved, the State Library of Kansas contracted with the University of Kansas to conduct an independent evaluation of the effectiveness of **6 by 6** in childcare settings.

The study was initially designed to be a five-year longitudinal study of the language gains of children. However, finding ongoing funding proved to be difficult, so State Library and university staff currently have preliminary findings from a two-year pilot study. A total of seven libraries, 102 children, and 20 childcare programs were enrolled in the two-year pilot.

The researchers reported several significant findings:

- Inviting small groups of childcare providers to the library for a brief **6 by 6** training session presented by library staff is an effective way to give early literacy information to community members.
- A short provider training at the library is as effective as three to four teaching outreach visits to childcare programs. Researchers recommended that local libraries in Kansas continue to offer **6 by 6** introductory meetings to small groups of childcare providers in their areas.
- Six months after attending meetings at their libraries, childcare providers reported using the library more often, including checking out materials for use with children in their care.
- Children's reading readiness increased approximately two months after their caregivers were introduced to **6 by 6**. Children continued to show gains when assessed four months later.

State Library staff have made these findings known to the Kansas library community and provide any interested Kansas libraries with the materials needed to present this type of outreach program in their communities.

was as effective as three to four teaching outreach visits to childcare programs. So with a small amount of coordination and preparation, library staff can train several childcare providers in one session at the library, as opposed to making many separate visits to each of those childcare providers in their centers or homes.

Researchers also found that having even this brief contact with their libraries increased providers' library use, including the providers accessing more materials for the children in their care.

This means that your library staff can have an effective impact on your community with a minimal amount of staff time, which is good news in these days of strained budgets and time-constrained staff members.

Checkup and Check Out: For Kansas Kids

Shortly before Anna began working as the state's early literacy coordinator, staff from the Kansas Pediatric Foundation approached the State Library about forming a partnership to better provide early literacy resources to Kansas children and families. Both agencies serve families with children up to age six and work throughout the state, so a partnership seemed logical and potentially of great benefit to Kansas families.

Anna met with Mel Hudelson, associate director of the Pediatric Foundation, and the two came up with a simple outreach program that libraries could conduct with local clinics, Checkup and Check Out: For Kansas Kids. With Checkup and Check Out, in addition to giving out literacy advice at well-child checkups for children ages six months through five years, physicians give families information about **6 by 6** and encourage them to visit their local library to learn more about early literacy.

Clinicians also give families vouchers to take to the library to receive an additional book to add to their home libraries. Libraries receive grant money from the State Library to purchase books for distribution to participating families. The initial phase of Checkup and Check Out included four Kansas communities, and the program has since expanded to 12 communities, including urban, suburban, and rural areas.

The program's goal was to bring new families into the library, and that goal is being met. When families come to the library to select their Checkup and Check Out books, the adults are asked to complete a voluntary survey. For the first complete year of the program, just over 25 percent of survey respondents said that their first visit to the library was to pick up their child's Checkup and Check Out book. In addition, nearly 30 percent of respondents said they had been to the library with their children only one to five previous times.

Implications for Outreach

The goal of outreach activities is twofold. First, if you have the drive and passion for bringing library services to those who cannot access them, providing services such as outreach storytimes at child education centers can be an important part of your early literacy efforts.

Second, special things happen *at* the library, so invite as many people through your library's doors as possible—in whatever ways you can. This is the intent of programs like Checkup and Check Out.

Of course, your library may not have the financial resources to give brand-new picture books away to families. But giving children books builds goodwill with families, and our library staff members always report enjoying this task very much. Look for other options—perhaps your Friends group could provide a grant of funds or conduct a drive for high-quality, gently used picture books that could be used to support such an effort. Other premium incentives would work well, also. You could have staff and community members record songs and rhymes, and DVDs and CDs can be replicated fairly inexpensively.

Giving out those incentives also gives your library staff a chance to start a conversation about the resources the library has to offer the families who come in to collect them. Instruct all staff members to sign families up for library cards and give them a tour of the library and a calendar of events (as time allows).

Looking Ahead

This chapter has addressed the details of establishing and tailoring an early literacy program to meet the needs of individual communities, and we've explained the importance of outreach, including some effective outreach methods. In the next chapter, you'll take a closer look at meeting the early literacy needs of people who use your library.

References

McLellan, Kathy, in discussion with Bradley Debrick, March 2015.
Riley, Kasey Laine, personal communication with the authors, March 2015.

Chapter 3

Helping Children Learn the Six Skills, and Helping Adults Help Children

This chapter addresses the issues and opportunities library staff members may encounter in presenting early literacy concepts and experiences in your library. It is divided into three main sections covering early literacy in storytimes, in activity spaces, and in speaking with adults. Each of these situations presents a unique set of opportunities to share early literacy information and experiences with your community.

In the Library: Storytimes

Many libraries use traditional terminology for their programs like Baby Time, Toddler Time, or Preschool Time, which for the most part parallel the age groups **Early Talker**, **Talker**, and **Pre-Reader**. Some libraries have created unique names for their storytimes like Book Babies, or Storytime Explorers. You should use whatever titles are effective at getting the right ages into your programs. When talking specifically about **6 by 6**, you may want to use the research terminology and tie it to your storytime names. For example, "Children ages three to six are considered **Pre-Readers** and that is the perfect audience for our Storytime Explorers program on Tuesday and Thursday mornings."

Having a conversation with a caregiver who brings a baby to a program designed for four-year-olds can be difficult. However, it is a conversation that must take place. Explain, as gently as possible, that the stories and activities were selected for older kids, and a baby would likely be frustrated or bored. If that approach meets resistance, offer the caregiver a spot in the back of the room where they can slip out quietly if the baby gets fussy. If issues like this are frequent, or you don't have the time or staffing to offer age-specific storytimes, you may want to consider labeling your programs as "family" storytime. Family storytimes can be especially effective in small libraries. More about family sessions later in this chapter.

Storytime Groups

Early Talkers

These storytimes are most appropriate for children birth to two years and are often called Babytime, Baby Storytime, or Lap Sit Storytime. While we say these programs are for babies, they are actually for caregivers. You are modeling behaviors for them to repeat at home. Action rhymes or tickle rhymes may be unfamiliar or even uncomfortable for some adults, so your presentation gives them vital experience and information. During storytime, talk to the caregivers about why you chose a specific book or why songs and rhymes are important (rhythm of speech, rhyming words, bonding, shared experience). Show how to read a book with a baby, or demonstrate that it's even okay not to read the text but just talk about the pictures.

For **Early Talkers**, repetition helps establish the expectation for storytime for both the adult and the child, and builds their confidence. Repeating some songs or books week after week helps caregivers become comfortable with your patterns so they can focus on the important interactions with their babies. Babies are not the only ones who find routines comforting!

Talkers

These storytimes are most appropriate for children two and three years old. They are often called Toddler Storytime. Some children wish to sit away from their adults, but many young **Talkers** may wish to stay in the comfort of their caregivers' laps. That's perfectly fine, of course, because we want children to be comfortable and have a good library experience. Time and time again, children who are shy at the start of a storytime session are often the ones who race into the room ready to get started just a few weeks later. Having children and caregivers sit in pairs also allows the adults to immediately practice the early literacy skills you demonstrate at storytime.

Your program plan can include stories with a more clearly defined narrative, simple fingerplays, and movement activities. Repetition still plays an important role with this group and helps the young audience build confidence with the repeated story or song. You may also want to introduce other methods of storytelling to them, such as puppets, flannelboards, magnet boards, big books, and audience participation stories.

Pre-Readers

These storytimes are most appropriate for children three, four, and five years old, and are often called Preschool Storytime. The older audience for these storytimes gives you great flexibility in demonstrating and developing the six skills. These youngsters can appreciate—and mostly sit still during—longer stories, which gives you the opportunity to talk about sequences and to introduce new vocabulary. Most of these children like to sing, which is an important part of the **Take Time to Rhyme** skill. Many children already know their alphabet at these ages, which means they have already begun to master the **Look for Letters** skill.

While this could be considered an independent experience where the caregiver is allowed to browse the library while their child is in storytime, encourage adults to stay in the room—you continue to model behavior and deliver early literacy messages to the caregivers as you transition from one part of storytime to the next.

Family Storytime

As previously noted, many libraries have supplemented their age-specific storytime schedule with a storytime for everyone called "Family Storytime." These programs obviously require a bit more planning and flexibility from the storyteller since the composition of the audience is unknown until people walk in the door. Three important tips for planning family storytime are (1) overprepare; (2) when in doubt, choose simple stories; and (3) focus on **Have Fun With Books**. Johnson County Library offers family storytimes mostly evenings and weekends and maintains a robust age-specific schedule on weekday mornings. Experiment with various days and times to find out what works best for your community.

When planning family storytime, opt for simple books, rhymes, and songs. Ones at the **Talker** level are "middle ground" and will allow everyone to enjoy storytime. As a presenter, it is far easier to make a plan that is too simple more challenging for the group than vice versa. If you plan for material at the **Talker** level and almost all the children who show up are **Pre-Readers**, simply ask more questions as you read, and ask participants to try the songs and rhymes faster and faster. **Pre-Readers** and their adults will enjoy the challenge!

Special Groups

You may occasionally need or want to provide special storytimes for specific groups in your community such as childcare centers, homeschool cooperatives, families with special needs children, Mothers of Preschoolers playgroups, and bilingual families. This gives you a great opportunity to show the library's relevance to that audience at hand. It will also give you a chance to promote the many services and programs that the library offers besides storytime.

If a member of a group asks for a storytime, be sure to find out the ages of the children, how many there will be, how many caregivers to expect, and if there is a specific reason they are requesting the program. It's nice (but certainly not necessary) to accommodate special topics with your storytime. For example, if a preschool is visiting for Earth Day, you might perform a session on sharing, emphasizing that the library is green because members of the community share resources. Or perhaps the group has some new children in the program—a session on friendship and inclusiveness would certainly appeal to adults and children alike.

Storytime Basics

Framework

Over time, performers develop their own storytime framework that works for them. It's a strange concept for a nonlibrary person, but storytime is an intensely personal program! It is nearly impossible for one person to plan a storytime and another person follow the plan with the same enthusiasm. That being said, you will encounter 18 storytime plans in chapters 4–9 of this book. They are suggested as plans into which you can insert your own opening and closing process, rhymes, and songs. Feel free to adapt all of these plans and make them your own!

Opening

There are as many ways to gather kids together as there are minutes in a day. You may already have your favorite method. Using the same method or routine week after week helps kids "switch gears" and get into a storytime frame of mind. An easy-to-learn gathering song will serve you well—kids who are seated will sing with you while other kids continue to arrive.

Room Arrangement

Consider the audience perspective when setting up your room. For **Early Talkers**, having plenty of space for caregivers and babies to move around is crucial. Some might even bring blankets on which to sit, so be prepared for that if you are in a small room. If possible, designate a parking area for strollers. This is especially necessary if your room is small.

For **Talkers** and **Pre-Readers**, try focusing where the children sit by placing your chair in a corner and having the kids sit in an arc in front of you. Some libraries provide carpet squares on which the children sit. This method works great in a small storytime and gives each child his or her own space. In any case, you'll want a few adult-size chairs along the back edge of your space for caregivers who aren't able to sit on the floor. After all, since you are encouraging adults to stay in the room, make them comfortable. Chairs along the back edge also help define the storytime space and keep everyone focused, particularly in large rooms or open areas.

It may sound like overkill, but consider buying an inexpensive vacuum to keep the floor clean in your storytime area. A clean storytime area is a comfortable storytime area.

Materials and Manipulatives

If at all possible, have your materials within easy reach before you begin. Smooth transitions from one portion of storytime to the next minimize the risk of losing your audience's attention. With **Early Talker** and **Talker** storytimes, be sure your puppets and other fun-looking things are placed on a high table or concealed in some way to prevent curious hands from latching onto your materials when you're in the middle of something else! Use this same method for manipulatives you may choose to use during or after storytime, as well. Egg shakers, ribbon dancers, hoops, safety mirrors, and musical instruments can all be kept covered in a basket until time to be passed out. With babies and toddlers, out of sight is truly out of mind. Inviting young children up to the basket to pick up and return manipulatives does take a little extra time, but the interaction children have with each other and the storytime performer is invaluable.

Registration

When people register for an event—even if it is free—the event has a greater perceived value. Obviously, taking registration allows you to control the number of people who attend. But it also helps you ensure the right ages are attending each program, allows you to plan ahead for handouts and manipulatives, and can be used to remind caregivers or inform them of schedule changes. (Be aware of your library's privacy policy before collecting the e-mail addresses or phone numbers of your patrons.) Some libraries offer self-serve registration with online software, and others take manual registration in person and over the phone.

Registration, however, takes a lot of staff time, especially if you are offering multiple storytimes each week. If you do not want to take registration but are concerned about overcrowding, consider handing out tickets 10–15 minutes before storytime begins. You can purchase inexpensive rolls of carnival tickets or make your own laminated ones to use again and again. It is up to you how many tickets you make available. Perhaps you want only 12 **Early Talkers** but are comfortable with 40 **Pre-Readers**. You will find the audience size that works best for you. Be sure to take into account that the quality of the program may diminish if the audience gets too large.

An almost more perplexing problem than overcrowding is low attendance. It's usually impossible to assume what will or will not affect your attendance. A rainy day can keep people away or drive them in. But so can a sunny day. If you have perpetually low attendance for a registered storytime, try eliminating the registration so patrons feel more flexibility to attend when they can.

Consider giving your regular attendees small, business-card-size handouts printed with your storytime information so they have a convenient way to invite others. Old-fashioned community bulletin boards may be effective especially in kid-friendly places like grocery stores and casual restaurants. Johnson County Library worked with a small, locally owned restaurant to design a **6 by 6** place mat. One side of the place mat featured the restaurant's kids' menu and a word search for older kids. The reverse had a few early literacy activities, along with library locations and hours. The restaurant provided crayons for families to use.

Handouts

Caregivers generally appreciate handouts that help them learn and recite the rhymes you use in storytime. These can be very simple half-sheets that you create weekly, or more complicated booklets given at the start of the session that contain a variety of rhymes you plan to use. In lieu of handout, some storytellers prepare electronic images and project them on a screen so caregivers—especially those with **Early Talkers** or **Talkers** sitting in their laps—can recite the action rhymes and interact with their children without bumbling with a piece of paper. Some libraries use locally developed apps and tablets to share storytime rhymes with their patrons.

Food

Inevitably, some caregivers will bring snacks into storytime for their own children. Formulate your own opinion of this before it happens. There are several things to consider including respectfulness, messiness, and the potential food allergies of other children. There is no harm in allowing snacks, of course, but inform caregivers that the policy may change if the snacks become distracting or if you are made aware of a child with heightened allergies.

In the Library: Early Literacy Spaces

Many caregivers in your community may not be able to bring their children to storytime at the library. Family schedules, library programming schedules, and preschool schedules can all get in the way. Providing a patron-directed activity space is an excellent way to enhance your young patrons' early literacy experience.

These spaces allow caregivers and children an opportunity to develop pre-reading skills through play. The library can use a child's natural curiosity and motivation to provide semiformal activities that support one or more pre-reading skills.

Activities in these spaces need not be guided by a library staff member, but can be guided by the caregiver with simple instructions or suggestions posted near the play materials. Since these spaces are not reliant on the library's programming schedule, they are a huge benefit for families who cannot attend a regular storytime. Furthermore, they can be inexpensive and easily scalable for various sized libraries.

Facilities across Kansas have created **6 by 6** Early Literacy Spaces that range from a few simple manipulatives in a plastic shoebox to dedicated rooms filled with a dozen or more elements. Just as spaces vary, so do the activities. Some are as simple as ready-made retail items like wooden puzzles that help develop sequencing skills, or library-made magnets that encourage caregivers and children to match rhyming words. Once the activities are purchased or created, the space requires only a small amount of staff time throughout the day to maintain. These activity spaces have become an integral part of **6 by 6** in Johnson County to the point where some libraries have become family destinations.

Before you can have a successful activity space, you need to make room for it in your library and create the activities that will be included. Regardless of the size of your library, the quickest option to make room for an activity space is weeding and shifting your collection. Weeding is painful for some people, but, as has been stated for years in library literature, a current and fresh-looking collection will benefit your library in a number of ways—including allowing you to reclaim underutilized space for literacy activities!

Even if your shelving is fixed in place, the newly vacated stacks could provide an area for lightweight bins containing puzzles, games, or other manipulatives that support your early literacy efforts. Caregivers and children simply take a bin, interact with the materials (and with each other), and put the bin back with they are finished. Additionally, displaying age- and skill-appropriate books near the activities draws unmistakable parallels between early learning and your library's collection.

In addition to weeding and shifting, you may have other options depending on the size of library in which you work.

A Space Overhaul in a Larger Library

If you have a dedicated storytime room or youth programming space but not an area you can dedicate wholly to literacy activities, you could employ the same lightweight bins mentioned above and use a book cart to wheel them in after your storytime. This method can be quite effective because your target audience is already in place, you have a rapport with them, and you are right there to facilitate caregiver-child interaction. Think of this option as a slightly more intentional version of the hoops, bubbles, scarves, or ribbon dancers many children's librarians offer as "storytime extenders." By providing as few as three different early literacy activities, you are giving kids a choice in their own learning and possibly appealing to a learning style that a traditional storytime does not. If practical, after your final storytime of the day, leave this room open for other library families to enjoy.

If your library has both a storytime room and a meeting room, it may be feasible to change your routine and offer storytime in the meeting room and convert your storytime room into a full-time early literacy activity space. That's just what the Antioch branch in Johnson County did in 2009. The building housed the library system's largest public meeting room, but it was minimally used on weekday mornings. A corner of the room was decorated for storytime, which made a spacious and comfortable area for the growing number of attendees. For **Early Talker** and **Talker** storytimes, tables and chairs were used to create a boundary that not only made the space feel cozier, but helped contain the highly mobile audience.

The former storytime room was refreshed with bright paint and repurposed as the very first **6 by 6** early childhood literacy activity space. In 2014, the 300-square-foot early literacy activity space averaged 4,300 door counts per month.

In libraries that have ample floor space and accommodating budgets or donors, interactive early learning stations are another option. These are not iPad holders mounted to an end panel; they are specially designed, museum-quality installations. A leader in this field is Burgeon Group in Phoenix, whose talented craftspeople work exclusively with public libraries and understand how play builds a foundation for pre-reading. With grant money from a variety of sources, Johnson County Library has been able to install attractive, durable, customized, and wildly popular Burgeon units in 6 of the 13 locations.

Creating a Medium-Size Early Literacy Space

Flexibility is important in designing a medium-size early literacy space. First of all, as mentioned above, try to be flexible with your storytime area: storytime

This early literacy interactive unit was custom-designed by the Burgeon Group in Phoenix, AZ. © Burgeon Group, LLC.

for part of the day, literacy activities for the rest of the day. In a medium space, you'll likely have enough room for at least a few pieces of child-size furniture. Attempt to choose furniture that can do double and triple duty. For example, a small work table with storage bins underneath. The tabletop can, of course, be used for anything that needs a workspace, such as puzzles, matching games, or pre-writing tasks. The bins underneath are perfect for holding activities that have multiple parts along with a small sign or laminated sheet with the activity instructions. Children and caregivers simply choose a bin, set it on top of the table for play, and return the bin underneath when they are finished.

Also, don't overlook existing elements in your library that might have an unexpected purpose. Steel shelving end panels are perfect for magnetic letter, shape, and sequencing activities, and child-height bulletin boards covered with felt become interactive storytelling canvases. Check your local fire code (and with your supervisor, of course!) but you may also consider using T-pins to hold shapes, letters, or sequencing objects to the acoustic tile in the ceiling.

A Space Conversion in a Small Library

In some libraries, particularly small ones, a dedicated early literacy space may not be possible. You may have a hard time finding enough space for a single activity let alone floor space for a set of activities, not to mention finding storage for tubs when the activities are not in use. Sandra Wilkerson, children's consultant with Southeast Kansas Library System, has helped many libraries in her area implement **6 by 6**. In e-mail correspondence with the authors, she said that many of her libraries have space issues and that "this means the activities that are displayed rotate or move around the library. The kids seem to find their space, even if you move it from place to place."

A small 400 square foot area in Edgerton, KS holds the library's entire youth collection and early literacy activities. © Burgeon Group, LLC.

Even with floor space at a premium, there are examples of small libraries creating dedicated activity spaces. In Norcatur, Kansas (population 151), Library Director Betsy Jakowski created a children's room out of a cluttered storage closet. She was inspired by the **6 by 6** artwork to create a colorful, inviting space for children to look at books and work on early literacy activities with their adults. To help fill the shelves that line the room, Betsy sought donations and grant funding to expand the library's selection of children's materials. The early literacy room has a very small reading nook in one corner, and because there is no space for a table, Betsy uses the ends of the shelves as workspaces for early literacy activities.

If neither of those options would work in your situation, consider developing early literacy "play packs" no larger than a lunch box. Each pack could contain two or three things to do: a small puzzle, nesting blocks, a magnetic drawing board, bead tracking toy, wooden cars, shape-matching dominoes, and the like. These play packs take up minimal space in a file cabinet and can be pulled out whenever an appropriately aged child needs something to work on. For example, if a caregiver needs 15 minutes to complete an online job application, provide a play pack to the child so he or she can be quietly engaged. Even though you won't have the adult-child interaction upon which **6 by 6** hinges, you'll at least give the child something to do that improves coordination and creativity.

What's Play Got to Do with It?

The benefits of play in early childhood cannot be overstated. There are many definitions of play, but there are two that seem to work best when thinking about early literacy play in the library. The first definition is by David Elkind from his book, *The Power of Play*. He states, "During infancy and early childhood, play is the dominant and directing mode of activity."

Using that definition, we can assume that when young children visit the library with their caregivers, they will be playing. It's a young child's dominant activity. The library can capitalize on a child's natural tendency to play by providing appropriate activities, toys, and manipulatives. If those activities, toys, and manipulatives happen to enhance pre-reading skills, all the better!

A second definition that strongly supports adding play to the public library comes from the Welsh government. (A number of European countries seem to be ahead of the United States in recognizing the benefits of play.) The Welsh General Assembly adopted a national Play Policy in 2002, which defines play as behaviors that are "freely chosen, personally directed, and intrinsically motivated." Not only does that definition perfectly describe everything we want our children's areas to be, but it also describes excellent public library service as a whole.

In recent years, dozens of articles and books have been written bemoaning the changing face of play or the disappearance of it altogether. Why the general agreement that play is necessary? What exactly does play accomplish?

According to the editors of *Children's Play: The Roots of Reading*, play allows children to:

- Self-motivate,
- Self-regulate,
- Explore,
- Problem solve,
- Interact/dialogue,
- Experiment,
- Build confidence, and
- Develop personal ethics.

As professionals in our field, we should find ways to harness that play—activities kids are doing naturally—and focus it into a framework for later learning. Libraries across Kansas are using the activity spaces mentioned above to encourage adult-child interactions that look and feel like play—and they are. But they also help children develop early literacy skills.

Not all kinds of play are appropriate in public libraries, of course. What has proven itself time and time again is semiformal play where the library provides manipulatives and a suggestion for their use, but ultimately allows children to play in whatever way they desire. This is not the time for formal, product-oriented craft making or traditional coloring sheets. These activities should be flexible enough to accommodate a variety of ages and stages and also be engaging enough to make caregivers want to participate. When an adult and child work together, that's when magic happens.

When brainstorming for your early literacy space and activities, get your whole staff involved in the planning. If they have input and understand the goal of the space, odds are you won't be tackling the project alone. Remember to discuss your library's tolerance for noise and behavior. The activity space can be loud especially right before and after storytime. Discuss noise levels with your public service staff in advance so that expectations are the same for all patrons throughout the day.

Here are some play-based activities we found ourselves using again and again because they are basic, effective, and easy to relate to various themes. These types of activities have been used in the **6 by 6** activity spaces in various sized public libraries. This list is not exhaustive but provides a good overview of what has proven successful:

Blocks

In addition to building literacy skills, block play allows children to explore math and science concepts and work collaboratively with others. We especially like the water blocks available through Lakeshore Learning and have found them to be very durable. And because they come in various shapes and have transparent liquid centers of various colors, they are excellent prompts for discussing shapes and color mixing.

Book Play

Using books for a purpose other than reading. For example, using three books to build a house for a set of toy animals.

Dramatic Play

Acting out a familiar story with defined characters and actions.

Exploration

Playing with a new object for the first time, or playing with a familiar object in a different way. For example, using a muffin tin as a way to sort differently shaped objects.

Games

Games often encourage talking among the players. They can also be used to introduce taking turns and being respectful.

Matching

Finding objects that are the same or discussing objects that are different connects with letter knowledge and vocabulary development.

Pretend Play

Differs from dramatic play because there is no set script. This is semiformal play at its best. Many preschool classrooms dedicate space for pretend play by setting up a mini house, kitchen, office, or library.

Puppets

Storytelling is a powerful way to build literacy skills. When children play with puppets, they may engage with as many as five or six of the early literacy skills. Puppets encourage imaginative play, which is essential to children's social and emotional development. Relevant puppets may also encourage children to retell the story they have recently heard, which is a great way for them to learn to **Tell Stories About Everything**.

Puzzles

Putting together a puzzle is a sequence of events that supports learning narrative skills. It is also a lesson in shape matching, which helps build letter knowledge. Puzzles are excellent ways for children to experiment with spatial relationships, a skill that is crucial in decoding text and in learning how to form letters. We frequently display puzzles that relate to the current theme.

Simple puzzles help **Early Talkers** and **Talkers** develop sequencing skills and shape recognition.

Reading

Reading is the obvious activity on this list. One great joy of working in a library is finding the right book for the right child at the right time. Keep them having fun and they will be motivated to learn to read!

Rhyming

Poems, songs, tongue twisters. Generally, listening for words that sound alike.

Rich Language

Rare, unusual, or Tier 2 words: these are words that kids do not hear very often in regular conversations, but do encounter in print form. Rare words help develop a rich vocabulary.

Sequencing

Putting objects in order and recognizing when something is not in the proper order.

Singing

Kids are naturally drawn to music and rhythm. This helps them break words apart and hear the rhymes.

Talking

Narrating tasks or describing activities or objects in detail. A great way to build vocabulary and narrative skills in children.

Texture Play

Children can first use their sense of touch and then their expanding vocabulary to describe what they feel. A dollop of fingerpaint sealed in a zip-top bag will allow children to push the paint around with their fingers to make lines, scribbles, or, for older children, letters. This is not only texture play, but is a pre-writing activity. Consider double-bagging the paint and sealing the edges with packing tape to improve the durability. These are known as "goo bags" in our libraries and are immensely popular with patrons. Other fun textures to touch and describe include sandpaper, Bubble Wrap, smooth stones, wood, non-skid shelf liner, wallpaper samples, fabrics, wicker, duct tape, carpet remnants, and seashells. Texture and other sensory play activities can be especially beneficial for children with special needs.

Tracking

Our eyes track across the page as we read a book. Kids can develop this fine motor skill by moving their hands and following them with their eyes. Action rhymes are an excellent form of practice. We also frequently employ bead mazes in our early literacy spaces. These educational toys allow children to practice fine motor skills, which leads to the ability to write. In watching what they are doing, children develop eye-hand coordination, a crucial skill in reading and in writing.

Writing

Whatever stage of writing a child is in, it is important for him to know that the thoughts and ideas he has can be represented graphically on paper. Regular pencils, colored pencils, crayons, washable markers, and chalk have all been used effectively, and without incident, in Kansas libraries. We discuss pre-writing skills development in a separate section later in this chapter.

All of these activities can serve as learning-oriented play at your library, though perhaps not all at once! Be aware that some activities require more investment of supplies and staff time. Also, you may find some activities don't work well with your patrons (or it just takes a while for your patrons to understand their purpose).

Be prepared to see creative use of your space. Just because you intend for an activity to work a certain way doesn't mean that's how kids will want to play with it. As long as they are playing safely and not damaging your materials, "Let them play!"

For example, adults would think the magnetic letters in this image should be used to spell a word or to sort into alphabetical order.

Most of all, have fun with kids! Join them in playing, especially if their caregiver is hesitant to engage or is interacting with another child. The behaviors you model in your activity space are equally as important as the ones you model in storytime.

Intermix basic shapes (and random shapes) with letters for play.

Early Literacy Activity Kits
Development

While some librarians are moving away from storytime themes, it may still be helpful for your first few activity kits to be themed around a popular picture book. Choose a book that kids enjoy, one that inspires you to be creative, and one that is in print or otherwise readily available. Other considerations include available formats (board book, e-book, audiobook), languages other than English, and whether the book is a good read-aloud. There may be times when you could plan a kit around a special event like an upcoming author visit or a "One State, One Book" type of celebration. Each November is designated as Kansas Reads to Preschoolers Month, with the goal of having every Kansas child hearing the selected title. Johnson County Library and the State Library of Kansas have worked for the past several years to make available activity kits based on the selected title.

Here is a list of books for which early literacy activity kits have been developed in the state of Kansas:

- *Alphabet Under Construction*, by Denise Fleming
- *Blue Sea*, by Robert Kalan
- *Chicka Chicka Boom Boom*, by Bill Martin Jr.
- *Click Clack Moo*, by Doreen Cronin
- *Dog's Colorful Day*, by Emma Dodd (prepared for Kansas Reads to Preschoolers Month, 2013)
- *Freight Train*, by Donald Crews
- *How Do Dinosaurs Say Goodnight?*, by Jane Yolen
- *I'm the Biggest Thing in the Ocean*, by Kevin Sherry
- *Is Everyone Ready for Fun?*, by Jan Thomas (prepared for Kansas Reads to Preschoolers Month, 2014)
- *Looking Like Me*, by Walter Dean Myers (prepared for Mr. Myers' visit to Johnson County Library, 2013)
- *Mushroom in the Rain*, by Mirra Ginsburg
- *Pete the Cat: I Love My White Shoes*, by Eric Litwin
- *Press Here*, by Hervé Tullet
- *Put It On the List!*, by Kristen Darbyshire
- *The Real Mother Goose*, illustrated by Blanche Fisher Wright
- *Seven Blind Mice*, by Ed Young
- *Snowballs*, by Lois Ehlert
- *Tip Tip Dig Dig*, by Emma Garcia
- *Underground*, by Denise Fleming (prepared for the Collaborative Library Summer Program theme "Dig Into Reading," 2013)
- *The Very Hungry Caterpillar*, by Eric Carle

As mentioned elsewhere in this book, achieving buy-in from library staff is key to the success of any library initiative, including **6 by 6**. One way of garnering staff support for your activity space is to get everyone involved in the creation of the activities. Put a copy of your chosen book in a staff area along with a suggestion box or a dry-erase board. Encourage staff to read the book and suggest activities that connect with the six skills (you may want to post the early literacy skills as a reminder).

Of course, your master list of activities will likely include ideas you've found on the Internet and some you've created yourself, but allowing your coworkers to take part in this creative process makes them feel included, and you'll likely be surprised at the creative ideas you get. This type of collaboration across departments or roles can be beneficial. Imagine how that part-time library page will feel when she sees a child interacting with an activity she suggested!

Once you have your master list of activity ideas, you'll need to pare it down to those activities that are viable and affordable. Consider your patrons and their behavior when you make your decisions. For example, what will your patrons do with washable markers? Will you end up with scribbles everywhere, or will the caregivers be able to direct children toward appropriate use?

And what about wooden puzzles? Will your custodian find pieces scattered all over the library, or will your patrons understand the need to keep everything in its place? Be prepared for your young patrons' creativity, too! Just because you want kids to pretend your pail of loofah sponges is a bucket of snow doesn't mean they will!

Simple signs help adults make the most of the learning opportunities in the library activity spaces.

A general rule of thumb: if kids aren't damaging the items, hurting themselves or others, or preventing other patrons from enjoying the library, it's probably productive play and should be tolerated. You may think of fantastic activities that simply cannot be left unsupervised (such as modeling clay, shaving cream, paint, process-oriented projects, and gross motor exploration). It is perfectly acceptable for you to use that activity only when staff or volunteers are available. If you have an established volunteer program, this is the perfect place for someone who wants to work with kids.

Signs in your activity space serve more than one purpose. Of course, they provide directions for play, but they can also give caregivers an idea as to how to use the materials most effectively. A simple sentence that connects your activity to early literacy is generally enough for a caregiver to make the connection, which in turn makes the play experience more meaningful.

Adaptation

A large kit with a dozen activities may not work in every library. That was the case in smaller libraries across Kansas. With feedback from regional directors and consultants, staff members from the State Library and Northwest Kansas Library System (NWKLS) adapted the kit program to include medium- and small-size kits. Mary G. Boller from NWKLS was a lead organizer in adapting the kits.

She says, "Many libraries use the early literacy activity kits as part of their passive programming." She recommends keeping this principle in mind even when assembling kits for very small libraries: "Create ideas, themes and activities that are first fun and creative for the children. The concepts and educational toys we included in the **6 by 6** kits allowed children the most basic access to creating and learning."

Medium kits are known as Circle Storytime Kits, and each is intended to be "storytime in a box": a themed set of six or more books, along with some type of storytime enhancer (puppets, music, flannelboards), and a binder of storytime resources (songs, booklists, action rhymes, and take-home handouts). Many of the kits contain more than six books because whenever possible, Boller included books on the themes appropriate for storytimes for **Early Talkers**, **Talkers**, and **Pre-Readers**.

The small kits are called Storypack Backpacks and their themes parallel the Circle Storytime Kits. These child-size backpacks include one book with a related activity (such as a puzzle or small flannelboard). These are intended to be loaned to families. The Storypack themes correlate to the Circle Storytime themes so that children can have an opportunity to take home a book that they have seen in storytime—or one similar to it—to further explore the theme and ideas they just experienced at the library.

All the kits (regardless of size) are made available to Kansas libraries through interlibrary loan. Libraries may choose to loan the medium and large kits to local childcare programs. By offering materials through interlibrary loan, grant funds are used efficiently and strategically.

Overall, the kits have been very well received by the Kansas library community. Library staff members have expressed appreciation for the ability to use high-quality resources at no charge. They have also reported using the kits to augment storytime, along with using them as stand-alone drop-in programs.

For Boller, the statewide kit project has been a huge undertaking, but one she finds worth the hours of effort she has dedicated to it. When asked why she and NWKLS Director George Seamon agreed to take on the kit project, Boller stated, "We know the direct correlation between early literacy and lifelong reading success. The tools, activities and resources included in each kit directly impact the reading success of Kansas children."

A Close Look at an Early Literacy Activity Kit

Each large early literacy activity kit contains the following:

- Several copies of the high-quality children's picture book the kit is centered on
- Materials for at least eight early literacy activities that relate to the selected book, with at least one activity for each of the six skills
- Signs to post that briefly explain how to do each activity and how each will help children learn at least one of the six skills
- Photos of each completely set up activity that help staff members know which materials belong with each activity

Let's take a detailed look at one of the large early literacy activity kits, one centered on *Tip Tip Dig Dig* by Emma Garcia. The signs posted for adults are composed of the words in the "title" and "message" fields below, along with the appropriate **6 by 6** character.

Activity A

Title: Put this shortened version of the story in order.

Message: Knowing that stories have a beginning, middle, and end is important for children who are ready to tell—and eventually read—stories.

Materials: Laminated copies of five pages from *Tip Tip Dig Dig*, representative of the beginning, middle, and end of the story.

Skill addressed: Tell Stories About Everything

Activity B

Title: Look at all this mess! What can we do with it?

Message: Make your own adventure playground (like in the book). Encourage children to talk about their creations by asking questions like "Who will use your playground?" and "What can you make with this?"

Materials: Pieces of string, yarn, bits of paper of various colors, glue sticks, green and brown paper for backgrounds.

Skill addressed: Tell Stories About Everything

Activity C

Title: Which machine do you like best?

Message: Write your name or draw a picture to cast your vote. Build children's vocabulary by talking about why a particular machine is your child's favorite.

Materials: sticky notes, pencils, a grid on the wall with picture of each type of machine at the top of the columns.

Skill addressed: Talk Talk Talk

Activity D

Title: Highway signs

Message: Use the road signs to create a safe highway. Noticing print in the environment isn't automatic. Point out road signs, follow the directions, and move the signs to other places on the roadway.

Materials: Highway mat or tape on the table or floor, small road signs, and play automobiles.

Skill addressed: Notice Print All Around You

Activity E

Title: Build a vehicle with these shapes.

Message: Recognizing shapes helps children learn to recognize letters.

Materials: Magnetic shapes and magnetic surface, or laminated paper shapes to use on a table, shelf, or floor.

Skill addressed: Look for Letters Everywhere

Activity F

Title: Tip Tip: Find two things that rhyme and put them in the truck.

Message: Rhymes help children learn to hear the smaller sounds of language, which helps them sound out words when they begin to read.

Materials: Toy dump truck(s), photos or toy replicas of rhyming items (such as cat and hat or tree and knee).

Skill addressed: Take Time to Rhyme, Sing and Play Word Games

Activity G

Title: Match traffic sign shapes: do any of them look like letters?

Message: Recognizing shapes is one of the steps in learning to distinguish among letters. As you sort the shapes, talk with your child about the names of the shapes.

Materials: Large traffic signs such as "Go," "Slow," and "Stop." Corresponding shapes to sort into baskets under the signs.

Skill addressed: Look for Letters Everywhere

Activity H

Title: Letters in the sand

Message: Gently move the bag and shake the sand to see the letters that are hidden inside.

Materials: Zip-top bag filled with plastic letters and sand, sealed and seams reinforced with book tape.

Skills addressed: Have Fun With Books, Look for Letters Everywhere

Activity I

Title: Tracks in the mud: gently roll the different wheels through the brown mud

Message: Holding and turning the wheels is difficult! It is also good practice for holding and turning the pages in a book.

Materials: Zip-top plastic bags, doubled up, filled with brown fingerpaint, sealed and seams reinforced with book tape. Rubber wheels from the hardware store.

Skill addressed: Have Fun With Books

These are the nine activities that are included in the early literacy activity kit for *Tip Tip Dig Dig.*

The Importance of Pre-Writing (in Kits and Everywhere)

With each activity kit you develop, be sure to include pre-writing and writing activities. This is an important—and at times overlooked—part of early literacy. In this book, the term "writing activities" refers to any activities that get children ready to write, such as the scribbling and drawing that **Talkers** do, and for **Early Talkers** even something as simple as handling objects. Touching and moving items helps children develop the gross and fine motor skills needed for handwriting and typing.

Include plenty of pre-writing and writing options in your activities. Design them with these principles in mind:

- Children start to learn writing skills at a very young age. All of the following lead to writing skills, so try to include as many as possible in your kits: gross motor skills, fine motor skills, hand-eye coordination, and, of course, any kind of mark making (scribbling, drawing, painting). With each theme, be sure to include writing activities for as many ages as possible.
- Writing should serve a purpose within the context of the theme, so strive for something more meaningful than a themed coloring page. For example, with *The Very Hungry Caterpillar*, we created a Caterpillar Café with picture menus and order pads so that children (or adults) could mark the food that was requested.
- Writing helps children make the connection between ideas and how they are represented in print. For *Put It on the List!*, one of the activities is to make a shopping list for lunch. The instructions for the activity encourage adults to have a conversation with children about what they want to eat and then make a list of the foods children say.

Pre-writing and writing activities fall into several categories, and thinking about them in the terms below will help you create varied activities for your early literacy spaces. There are many more ideas out there, but limit yourself to ones that are feasible in your library environment, where adults may or may not be closely monitoring their children.

Here are some pre-writing and writing possibilities to keep in mind when designing activities:

- Children seeing adults writing—list making, or drawing sheets with spaces for adults to write a caption and children's names, for example
- Drawing, scribbling, and writing with various implements—beyond pencil and crayon, if at all possible
- Making marks with fingers or with stamps on goo bags—these are described above

- Playing with peg boards, bead mazes, and puzzles to work on fine motor skills and hand-eye coordination—the eye tracking necessary for this type of coordination helps children with pre-reading in addition to pre-writing
- Tracing letters with fingers or with writing implements
- Making letter rubbings—cut letters out of sandpaper and provide patrons with paper and crayons to use
- Drawing letters using yarn, clay, or pipe cleaners

Consider Technology

We live in an increasingly screen-filled world. The previous recommendation by the American Academy of Pediatrics for no screen time for children under two is now unrealistic (and has been revised by the AAP). Here are two considerations to make when using technology with young children—whether at home or at the library:

- Use of technology should be selective and with a specific purpose.
- Use of technology should be interactive.

Purposeful Use

Consider technology as a tool you can use to achieve the best result. You don't need a hammer for every home improvement project, and you don't need to show a YouTube video at every storytime. When deciding to use technology in storytime or at the library, you should determine that it meets some learning needs children have.

Look at previews and check reviews to ensure you are downloading high-quality apps, music, videos, and books that will benefit children's learning. Some preview and review sources are suggested below. Be selective and purposeful with your use of technology, and advise families to do the same when they choose to use technology with their young children.

Interactive Use

Much of the discussion about technology use by young children focuses on the amount of time they spend viewing screens and using devices. Limiting children to a reasonable amount of screen time is important. However, even more important than the *amount* of time is the *quality* of that time. As with reading books, interaction is key.

Children will learn much more by using an interactive app than they will by simply watching a movie on a screen. The majority of apps on the market focus on alphabet knowledge and phonological awareness; however, you can find excellent apps that will support the other four pre-reading skills as well. And kids will learn much more if they have a caring adult interacting with the app with them.

We suggest following the recommendations made by Lisa Guernsey in her book *Into the Minds of Babes: How Screen Time Affects Children from Birth to Age Five*, to consider "The Three Cs" for your screen time use: the Child, the Content, and the Context in which it is viewed. Enjoying an app together creates an interactive and brain-engaging experience rather than a passive one.

Resources for Technology Use

For more detailed and up-to-date information on technology and young children, we recommend visiting the websites of the following organizations:

- Early Childhood Investigations (search the webinar archives for high-quality, informative sessions on tech and young children)
- Erikson Institute's TEC (Technology in Early Childhood) Center
- Fred Rogers Center
- The Joan Ganz Cooney Center at Sesame Workshop

For previews and reviews of electronic media for children, we recommend the following sources:

- Common Sense Media
- Demonstration videos on YouTube, the Play Store (Android) and the App Store (Apple)
- Little eLit

In the Library: Working and Speaking with Adults

A key to the success of any early literacy initiative will be getting library staff comfortable with the early literacy interactions they have with families, whether during storytime or during a regular day at the library. In your training sessions for library staff, stress that parents and caregivers want early literacy advice and that they see library staff as experts in the field.

In correspondence with the authors, NWKLS's Mary G. Boller noted, "Many libraries did not previously see themselves as a resource for parents and young children. They did not want to feel like they were trying to tell families what they needed to be doing. But access to books does not always translate to parents understanding what they can do to allow early success for their young readers. Through **6 by 6** I feel that librarians have come to see their role in early literacy intervention more clearly."

Melendra Sutliff Sanders, children's consultant for North Central Kansas Libraries System, concurs advising library staff to "get comfortable explaining what early literacy is and how the (recommended) activities enhance early literacy skills. Many parents do some of the things, and many of the parents do none of the things. As experts in early literacy practice, librarians need to be comfortable teaching parents the best ways to help their children. This means librarians need to do a lot of demonstrating (whether in storytime or during in-library activities)."

Caregivers who bring their children to the library already have some understanding of the importance of early experiences with books and reading. One of the goals for an early literacy program is to make those experiences an intentional part of everyday life, not just something done only during a routine visit to the library.

Encourage caregivers to attend storytime with their children so they can learn simple skills to replicate later when they are having lunch, sitting at a stop light, or waiting in the grocery store checkout line. When you build in short comments during your storytime that are directed to the caregivers (called "early literacy asides"), you can explain why you made the choices you did and how a particular book or action rhyme impacts a particular skill.

The efficacy of those asides was discussed in a 2014 article in *Children and Libraries*, the journal of the Association for Library Service to Children, and they are an important component of storytime. Early literacy asides help caregivers learn how storytime experiences lead to literacy development. (There are many examples of literacy asides in the storytime plans found in chapters 4–9.)

Even when families visit the library without a storytime scheduled, there are ways to make early literacy development possible. If your library still has an information or circulation desk, don't overlook those areas as an opportunity to engage your young patrons with early literacy.

A few puppets in a plastic shoebox or some type of interactive board mounted to the front of the desk will not only occupy a restless child while his caregiver works with library staff, but it will also get him active with storytelling, creative play, and fine motor development.

"Shelf talkers" are a convention retailers use to draw a shopper's attention to a specific product. Libraries can do the same to draw attention to particular sections or specific books. A variety of shelf talkers exist on the market and range from simple, single-use printables to reusable spring-operated aluminum clips.

A shelf talker near your board books could inform new parents about the importance of letting babies hold and handle books (**Have Fun With Books**). Another one near a display of wordless books could talk about the benefits of making up your own story as you read (**Tell Stories About Everything**).

Looking Ahead

Now that you have the framework for thinking about early literacy, how to talk to adults about it, and how to provide children with plenty of opportunities to explore it, let's consider each of the six skills in detail. Each of the upcoming chapters includes the following:

- Specific activities that help children develop the skill,
- Children's books that are especially good to explore the skill,
- How the skill relates to the others,
- How using the skill builds a foundation for lifelong learning, and
- Storytime plans and reproducible storytime guides for each of the three age groups.

References

Boller, Mary G., personal communication with the authors, March 2015.

Carle, Eric. *The Very Hungry Caterpillar*. New York: Philomel Books, 1994.

Cronin, Doreen. *Click Clack Moo: Cows That Type*. New York: Simon & Schuster Books for Young Readers, 2000.

Crews, Donald. *Freight Train*. New York: Mulberry Books, 1992.

Darbyshire, Kristen. *Put It on the List!* New York: Dutton Children's Books, 2009.

Dodd, Emma. *Dog's Colorful Day: A Messy Story about Colors and Counting*. New York: Dutton Children's Books, 2000.

Ehlert, Lois. *Snowballs*. San Diego: Harcourt Brace, 1995.

Elkind, David. *The Power of Play: How Spontaneous, Imaginative Activities Lead to Happier, Healthier Children*. Cambridge, MA: Da Capo Lifelong, 2007.

Fleming, Denise. *Alphabet Under Construction*. New York: Henry Holt, 2002.

Fleming, Denise. *Underground*. New York: Beach Lane Books, 2012.

Garcia, Emma. *Tip Tip Dig Dig*. London: Boxer, 2007.

Ginsburg, Mirra, and Jose Aruego. *Mushroom in the Rain*. New York: Macmillan Publishing, 1974.

Guernsey, Lisa. *Into the Minds of Babes: How Screen Time Affects Children from Birth to Age Five*. New York: Basic Books, 2007.

Kalan, Robert. *Blue Sea*. New York: Mulberry Books, 1992.

Litwin, Eric, and James Dean. *Pete the Cat: I Love My White Shoes*. New York: Harper, 2010.

Martin, Bill, and John Archambault. *Chicka Chicka Boom Boom*. New York: Simon & Schuster Books for Young Readers, 1989.

Myers, Walter Dean, and Christopher Myers. *Looking like Me*. New York: Egmont USA, 2009.

"Play Policy." Welsh Government. November 4, 2008. http://gov.wales/dcells/ publications/policy_strategy_and_planning/early-wales/playpolicy/playpolicye .pdf?lang=en. Accessed June 8, 2015.

Sanders, Melendra Sutliff, personal communication with the authors, March 2015.

Sherry, Kevin. *I'm the Biggest Thing in the Ocean*. New York: Dial Books for Young Readers, 2007.

Stewart, Roger, Stephanie Bailey-White, Staci Shaw, Erica Compton, and Saroj Ghoting. "Enhanced Storytimes: Effects on Parent/Caregiver Knowledge, Motivation, and Behaviors." *Children and Libraries* 12, no. 2 (2014): 9–13.

Thomas, Jan. *Is Everyone Ready for Fun?* New York: Beach Lane Books, 2011.

Tullet, Hervé. *Press Here*. San Francisco: Chronicle Books, 2011.

Wilkerson, Sandra, personal communication with the authors, March 2015.

Wright, Blanche Fisher. *The Real Mother Goose*. New York: Scholastic, 1994.

Yolen, Jane, and Mark Teague. *How Do Dinosaurs Say Goodnight?* New York: Blue Sky Press, 2000.

Young, Ed. *Seven Blind Mice*. New York: Philomel Books, 1992.

Zigler, Edward. *Children's Play: The Roots of Reading*. Washington, DC: Zero to Three Press, 2004.

Chapter 4

Have Fun With Books

Have Fun With Books is also known as Print Motivation in the early literacy field. Basically, it means children understand that reading and learning can be interesting and fun. Children who understand that reading can be enjoyable will be better motivated to do the complex brain work it takes to learn to read.

Enthusiasm: A Key to Learning This Skill

A key to fostering this skill in children is enthusiasm. If children see adults who are excited about reading and learning, children will get excited, too. Children who enjoy exploring stories and ideas naturally want to learn to read.

In addition to showing enthusiasm, adults who spend regular time with children understand when it's time to sit quietly and read a book, and when it might be more fun to sing a song and jump around. This is true of adult family members, educators, and library staff. If reading stops being fun—whether you're with a single child or a group—it's perfectly fine to stop reading and start singing, or just take a moment to talk about something interesting. In fact, it's preferable to do this!

And the opposite is true, too. Encourage adults to take books with them whenever they are with children. Looking at a book together while waiting in line at the grocery store can be a wonderful distraction and an excellent time to have fun reading together. In your library, you always have a selection of books at hand. Help parents and caregivers to do the same, no matter where they are.

Activities That Help Children Develop This Skill

- Show excitement for and during reading time.
- Explore all kinds of reading with children. Look at magazines, catalogs and child-friendly apps together. Read the labels and directions on household items.
- Ask questions about the pictures. If children are too young to answer, reply for them.
- Use fun facial expressions and voices while reading.
- Have children repeat common phrases with you . . . but Goldilocks said . . . "it's just right!"
- Show children that reading and writing are useful in daily life by looking at grocery ads together and making your shopping list, and then have them read recipes with you as you cook lunch or dinner together.
- Get picture books with little or no text so that children can read to you by telling stories about the pictures they see.
- Use books that encourage searching for objects in the illustrations—this is fun with an adult-child pair or with groups of children.

- Find ways to ensure children have books at home—give books as gifts, and ask for donations of books for the children you know.
- Create a personalized book for children. If they are old enough, ask them to help you tell the story about themselves. For younger children, talk with them about what they are doing, and show them you are writing down their activities. Have children participate in story making by illustrating their books.

Books That Are Very Good for Have Fun With Books

Note: Most high-quality picture books illustrate more than one skill. These just happen to be some favorites that help children learn this skill.

Actual Size, by Steve Jenkins
Jenkins uses cut-paper illustrations to show animals—or parts of animals—in their full, adult sizes. From the tiny pygmy mouse lemur to huge foot of the African elephant, children are enchanted by seeing animals in their true-to-life sizes. Some illustrations slip off the edges of the pages, like the goliath frog, making for an interesting talk about how books usually work, and how this one is different. Be sure to talk about the gatefold—it actually takes a three-page spread to show the size of a saltwater crocodile's mouth! Clear and bold illustrations make this a good book for storytime, and the interesting facts Jenkins presents means it also works well for individual and small group reading.

Alphablock, by Christopher Franceschelli
This chunky board book has few words, but children of all ages enjoy its clever design. Large die-cut letters provide a great chance to **Look for Letters**, and the letters give a clue as to what the next word will be. For example, N sits on a tree branch next to a bird with a twig in its mouth. "N is for . . . " (turn the page) "NEST." The short, single-word answers paired with clear illustrations will have **Pre-Readers** recognizing words by sight.

Bark, George, by Jules Feiffer
Pre-Readers are in on the joke as a well-meaning doctor extracts larger and larger animals from George's tummy. The facial expressions from George's mother, the uproariously silly story, and the surprise ending make this a no-fail title for print motivation.

Brown Bear, Brown Bear, What Do You See?, by Bill Martin Jr.
One of the quintessential storytime books. The repeating cadence and perfectly composed illustrations help the youngest of readers gain reading confidence. Print motivation achieved! Have children help turn the pages. Singing your way through this book adds another level of fun and helps with **Take Time to Rhyme**.

Chugga-Chugga Choo-Choo, by Kevin Lewis
So many children's books rhyme, and this one does, too. But it also features alliteration, meaning that some words begin with the same sound but end differently, like "chugga" and "choo." Alliteration is another way for children to learn to hear the smaller sounds in words. This title is also great for **Have Fun With Books** because children can participate in the story by sounding the train's whistle throughout the book.

Driving My Tractor, by Jan Dobbins
A farmer drives his tractor and wagon across the farm, picking up animals along the way. This book is packed with options for **Have Fun With Books** and **Take Time to Rhyme**. Children love chanting the repeated phrase "Chug, chug, clank, clank, toot! It's a very busy day" while reading the book. And the accompanying CD/DVD has an illustrated version of the story that encourages children to sing along. This title is also good for **Notice Print** because after the story ends, the book continues with some facts about farming, and the final page has the sheet music for the song.

Duck on a Bike, by David Shannon
Much to the chagrin of his barnyard companions, a fun-loving duck takes a ride on a bicycle. Not only is there an incredibly strong narrative from beginning to end, but each double-page spread has its own mini story. Why exactly is the cat so disinterested? Why is the horse so smug? Make this story interactive by asking children to help Duck greet the animals as he rides by. Near the end, you can spend time on the page with all the animals on bikes to try to recall the order in which the animals appeared in the story.

Go Away, Big Green Monster!, by Ed Emberley
This classic book uses die-cut pages to make a monster's face appear and then disappear, feature by feature. Children feel empowered to tell the monster to "Go away!" one feature at time. Exploring the names of facial features builds vocabulary for young children, and the die-cuts make for fun discussion of the shapes you can see in this book. This is a wonderful story for retelling by using a puppet, felt board, or pieces of paper. Be sure to check out Emberley's companion title, *Nighty Night, Little Green Monster*.

Huff & Puff: Can You Blow Down the Houses of the Three Little Pigs?, by Claudia Rueda
Many children are familiar with the story of the Three Little Pigs, but this simple book invites readers into the story to play the role of the Big Bad Wolf. Die-cuts in the pages show readers just where to huff and puff and blow houses down. Fortunately Wolf is unable to blow down the final house, but there is a surprise waiting inside. The various house construction materials give readers plenty to discuss. For example, why does the brick house stand when the others fell?

I Spy on the Farm, by Edward Gibbs
"I spy with my little eye . . . something red that begins with an R. Cock-a-doodle-doo!" Invite children to look through the hole and use the clues—color, letter, sound—to guess which animal will be revealed next. The interactive illustrations encourage young readers to play with the book by making animal noises and peeking through the cutouts. Be sure to check out the other titles in this series—they are all excellent.

Little Pea, by Amy Krouse Rosenthal
Oh, to be a little pea at dinnertime! Pea's parents require him to eat all of his candy before he can have his delicious dessert—a big bowl of spinach. This hilarious book provides a great motivation to enjoy reading, especially for picky eaters and the adults who love them.

The Napping House, by Audrey Wood
A classic cumulative tale in which nearly everyone is asleep . . . for a while at least. An abundance of rich words are placed carefully in this story: dozing, snoozing, dreaming, slumbering. The structure lets you hear those words over and over as you read. Try using some of these rare words in the daily conversations with children. This is a great title to have children read along with you, prompting them to repeat the phrase, "where everyone is sleeping." And because of the sharp contrast of the weather at the beginning and the end of this book, it's a great one to retell using three two-page spreads, one each from the beginning, middle, and end.

Moo, Baa, La La La!, by Sandra Boynton
In Sandra Boynton's classic title, some animals make their traditional sounds, and some do not. The thick lines and plain backgrounds are perfect for **Early Talkers** who will relish making animal noises right along with you as you read.

Pajama Time!, by Sandra Boynton
Even though the book centers around nighttime rituals, it's a fun read-aloud for anytime! Simple, bouncy rhymes that describe different kinds of pajamas and a repeating "Pajama Time!" refrain make this an excellent **Have Fun** book for your toddler.

Pete the Cat: I Love My White Shoes, by Eric Litwin
Pete is a modern classic. The catchy text invites singing along, and Pete's irrepressible attitude is engaging, encouraging readers to keep walking along and singing their songs. A variety of text features makes for an interesting discussion, especially with **Pre-Readers**. What is a thought bubble, and how is it different from regular print? What do those quotation marks tell us? And what about those musical notes on some pages?

Press Here, by Hervé Tullet
Simple instructions allow children to guide the action as colorful dots proliferate, move about, grow, and shrink on every page. This book works well for one-on-one

sharing or in a larger group. The final page asks the reader if they want to do it again. You can probably guess the answer you'll get.

Sam & Dave Dig a Hole, by Mac Barnett
Kids are in on the joke as they cheer and groan for these two tireless boys on their quest to find something spectacular. The subtle but important clues on the opening and closing spreads add to the fun and the discussion. The subtle details are great for a lap experience, but the larger-than-life mishaps also make this a winner for any storytime!

Stuck in the Mud, by Jane Clarke
"'Help! Help!' clucked the hen. 'My poor little chick! He's stuck in the mud . . . and the mud's deep and thick!'" With this panicked start, Hen enlists the help of barnyard neighbors to free her wayward son. A repeated phrase, "pushed and pulled again and again," lets young readers help tell the story, and all of that pushing and pulling makes this a fun story to retell by acting it out. Great rhymes and rhythms make this a good book for **Take Time to Rhyme** as well. The use of expressive fonts (for instance, the letters in "pushed" are close together, and those in "pulled" are far apart) makes this a good one to use to talk about **Notice Print All Around You**.

There Are Cats In This Book, by Viviane Schwarz
A playful page-turner that interacts directly with the reader. Follow these three friendly felines by lifting flaps and turning die-cut pages as they play with yarn, boxes, pillows, and fish. The cats tell you what to do every step of the way, just follow along. You'll like them as much as they like you.

The Watermelon Seed, by Greg Pizzoli
What child hasn't accidently swallowed a watermelon seed and panicked at the thought of vines growing from their ears? That's the destined fate of a little crocodile who swallows a seed while eating his favorite food. Children instantly relate to the drama and find much humor in the illustrated results of a melon sprouting from within.

Where in the Wild?: Camouflaged Creatures Concealed . . . and Revealed, by David M. Schwartz and Yael Schy
There's a lot to love about this animal poetry book. It's illustrated with wonderful photos, and gatefold pages lift out to reveal where the animal is hiding. Alongside the poems, the authors have included plenty of interesting facts on each animal. A very versatile book—good for reading one poem to start off a storytime, or for sitting as a pair or in a small group and exploring for a very long time. When you're done, check out the sequel.

Who Has These Feet?, by Laura Hulbert
Throughout this book, two-page spreads ask "Who has these feet?", with an illustration of animal feet. The following spread provides the answer in text and

picture, along with a simple fact about that animal's feet; for example, "A tree frog has sticky pads on its toes so it can stick to leaves." Readers have fun guessing which animal has which feet, and the mix of animals featured will help children build vocabulary and background knowledge.

See the last few pages of this chapter for storytime plans for babies, toddlers, and preschoolers that use some of these books.

Connecting the Skills

It's easiest, perhaps, to think of **Have Fun With Books** as an umbrella under which all five of the other skills sit—the idea being that it is easier for a child to appreciate stories, learn new words, understand the alphabet, recognize the importance of print, and listen for rhymes when that child is hungry for books and reading to begin with. Brain chemistry changes when children are learning in a positive, comfortable environment. The serotonin released acts as a "fixative" and can help kids remember and connect learning experiences. This is not the time for forceful and negative language. "Go to your room and read!" should not be a punishment. Instead, we want to encourage repeated, positive experiences with books and reading.

Have Fun With Books can be connected to **Take Time to Rhyme** by playing word games and reading silly, rhyming poetry. Singing songs—especially songs that have been written in book form or those with animal sounds—are great ways to have fun and listen for rhymes at the same time. **Look for Letters** can sometimes seem like a chore, but if you encourage shape play or "I spy" shape games it becomes a more engaging, challenging, and fun way to learn the alphabet. Children will start seeing shapes and letters everywhere and will be proud to point out each and every one.

Links to Lifelong Learning

No one should ever stop having fun with books. Just like we should never tire of a good story or stop adding words to our vocabulary. **Have Fun With Books** is a lifetime skill that begins with very early experiences. One goal of a librarian is to match the right book with the right reader. That process should start very, very early in a reader's life. Board books that babies can experience with all their senses (including taste!) get them comfortable with books and set up the understanding that books are an important part of life. As children develop more early literacy knowledge, they will take pride in their favorite book by turning the pages or telling a story using their own words. Kids on the upper age range for

6 by 6 will start writing and illustrating their own books during playtime. That is a true sign of high print motivation!

Storytime Plans for Have Fun With Books

The following section includes storytime plans for three age groups:

- **Early Talkers** (birth to approximately 18 months)
- **Talkers** (approximately 18 months to three years)
- **Pre-Readers** (approximately ages three to five years)

Adapt these plans to make them your own!

Have Fun With Books: A Storytime for Early Talkers

This plan is appropriate for children birth to 18 months old with a caregiver. Materials you will need for this storytime:

- Music and Songs:
  - "Peek-a-Boo" (Tune: "Frère Jacques")
  - "This Is the Way We Wave Hello" (Tune: "Here We Go 'Round the Mulberry Bush")
  - "Touch Your Toes" from *Diaper Gym*, by Priscilla Hegner and Rose Grasselli
  - "My Little Hands" from *Diaper Gym*, by Priscilla Hegner and Rose Grasselli
  - "Tummy Button" from *Wee Sing for Baby*©, by Pamela Conn Beall and Susan Hagen Nipp
  - "Brown Bear, Brown Bear, What Do You See?" from *Playing Favorites*, by Greg and Steve
- Action Rhymes:
  - "Tick Tock"
  - "Criss Cross Applesauce" from *The Kingfisher Playtime Treasury*, by Pie Corbett
- Books:
  - *Moo, Baa, La La La!*, by Sandra Boynton
  - *Pajama Time!*, by Sandra Boynton
  - *Brown Bear, Brown Bear, What Do You See?*, by Bill Martin Jr.

Call Everyone to Storytime

Use a rain stick or other simple instrument to gather everyone's attention, saying something like "Do you hear that? It's the sound of storytime. Time for storytime!" Once everyone is settled in place, introduce yourself and welcome everyone.

Give Opening 6 by 6 Message to Caregivers

Today is all about having fun. We want you and your child to enjoy reading books together and equate that book-sharing time with love and affection. Your baby's brain is developing rapidly in these first few years, so it's the perfect time to tell stories, sing, talk about pictures, and play. I am so happy you brought your baby to storytime today!

Sing the Welcome Song

"Peek-a-Boo" (Tune: "Frère Jacques")

> Peek a boo! Peek a boo!
> I see you! I see you!
> I'm so glad to see you! I'm so glad to see you!
> Peek a boo! Peek a boo!

Sing the Opening Song

"This Is the Way We Wave Hello" (Tune: "Here We Go 'Round the Mulberry Bush")

> This is the way we wave hello,
> Wave hello, wave hello.
> This is the way we wave hello
> So early in the morning!

Repeat with other actions such as clap our hands, touch our nose, tap our feet. Finish with wave hello once again.

Introduce and Read the Book

Moo, Baa, La La La!, by Sandra Boynton
    Point out title, author, and illustrator.

Deliver 6 by 6 Message to Caregivers

Even though this book is a little small to share in a group like this one, I am hopeful you can see how much fun it would be to share one-on-one. If not already, your child will soon be able to focus on the pictures. When that happens, you can pause and spend more time looking at and talking about the ones that seem to interest her the most.

Lead the Action Rhyme

"Tick Tock." Baby facing caregiver, caregiver holding baby just slightly in the air

> Tick tock, tick tock (swing baby side to side gently until the last line)
> I'm a little cuckoo clock
> Tick tock, tick tock
> Now it's almost three o'clock
> Cuckoo! Cuckoo! Cuckoo! (lift baby into the air on each "cuckoo")

Introduce and Play the Song

"Touch Your Toes" from *Diaper Gym*, by Priscilla Hegner and Rose Grasselli

Introduce and Play the Song

"My Little Hands" from *Diaper Gym*, by Priscilla Hegner and Rose Grasselli

Introduce and Read the Book

Pajama Time!, by Sandra Boynton

Deliver 6 by 6 Message to Caregivers

I mentioned earlier how quickly your baby's brain is developing. The whole chemistry of the brain changes when your baby (or anyone, for that matter!) is in a comfortable and happy environment. The serotonin released in the body helps the brain more easily retain those experiences and use them as the foundation for later learning.

Lead the Action Rhyme

"Tummy Button" from *Wee Sing for Baby©*, by Pamela Conn Beall and Susan Hagen Nipp.

> These are baby's fingers.
> These are baby's toes.
> This is baby's tummy button,
> Round and round it goes!
> These are baby's eyes.

This is baby's nose.
This is baby's tummy button,
Right where mommy blows!

Deliver 6 by 6 Message to All Participants

We are nearing the end of our storytime, so it's time for our final story and rhyme. I hope you will check out a few books to take home and find a bit of time every day to read together. If your baby gets fussy and doesn't want to stay calm, don't feel bad about putting the book down and trying again later. It doesn't have to be one long stretch of time, either. Just a few minutes here and there helps babies learn to love books.

Introduce the Book and Song

Brown Bear, Brown Bear, What Do You See?, by Bill Martin Jr. and "Brown Bear, Brown Bear, What Do You See?" from *Playing Favorites*, by Greg and Steve

This book is great to read aloud but can also be sung to a tune similar to "Baa Baa Black Sheep." We will listen to the song while I turn the pages.

Lead the Action Rhyme

"Criss Cross Applesauce." Begin with baby on lap, facing away from caregiver.

Criss cross applesauce (use finger to make X on baby's back)
Spiders crawling up your spine (crawl fingers up baby's spine)
Cool breeze (blow on baby's neck)
Tight squeeze (hug baby)
Makes you get the sillies! (tickle baby)

Invite Participants to Extend Storytime

Invite them to stay and explore your library's children's area.

Have Fun With Books: A Storytime for Talkers

This plan is appropriate for children approximately 18 months to three years old with their caregivers.

Materials you will need for this storytime:

- Music and Songs:
  - Rain stick or other simple instrument
  - "The More We Get Together" (sing or find a recorded version, such as Laurie Berkner's on the album *Buzz Buzz*)
  - "We Will Stomp," by Eric Litwin and Michael Levine, available online at The Learning Groove
  - "Storytime Is Over" (Tune: "If You're Happy and You Know It")
- Puppet:
  - Small mouse
- Poem:
  - "Hickory, Dickory Dock," traditional.
- Action Rhyme:
  - "Six in the Bed," abbreviated from the traditional "Ten in the Bed," many examples online
- Books:
  - *Go Away, Big Green Monster!*, by Ed Emberley
  - *The Napping House*, by Audrey Wood
  - *Stuck in the Mud*, by Jane Clarke

Call Everyone to Storytime

Use a rain stick or other simple instrument to gather everyone's attention, saying something like "Do you hear that? It's the sound of storytime. Time for storytime!" Once everyone is settled in place, introduce yourself and welcome everyone.

Give Opening 6 by 6 Message to Caregivers

Today's early literacy skill is **Have Fun With Books**. Children who enjoy books and reading will want to learn to read when it's time. Storytime is all about having fun with books, and during this session we'll talk about some ways to enhance the fun you can have with books whenever and wherever you read. We'll also preview some books that we'll use in future sessions when we feature the other skills

Sing or Play the Welcome Song

"The More We Get Together," traditional.

Note: Many adults are familiar with this song. If you use Laurie Berkner's recording and are not going to post all of the lyrics, be sure to make a poster with the names that Laurie sings in her version, so adults can continue to sing along.

Introduce the Puppet

Show the mouse puppet. Say that there will be a mouse in one of today's stories and that we will start with a poem about a mouse. Use the puppet to help illustrate the rhyme as you recite it.

Read/Recite the Poem

"Hickory Dickory Dock," traditional.

> Hickory dickory dock,
> The mouse ran up the clock,
> The clock struck one,
> The mouse ran down,
> Hickory dickory dock.
> Hickory dickory dock,
> The mouse ran up the clock,
> The clock struck two,
> The mouse said, "Boo!"
> Hickory dickory dock.
> Hickory dickory dock,
> The mouse ran up the clock,
> The clock struck three,
> The mouse said, "Whee!"
> Hickory dickory dock.
> Hickory dickory dock,
> The mouse ran up the clock,
> The clock struck four,
> The mouse said, "No more!"
> Hickory dickory dock.

Introduce the Book

Go Away, Big Green Monster! by Ed Emberley
    Point out title, author, and illustrator.

Deliver 6 by 6 Message to Caregivers

One way to show children books are fun is to have them participate in reading with you. As I read this book, I'll have you all help me say "Go away!" when it's time.

Deliver 6 by 6 Message to All Participants

In this story, a monster will appear. But don't worry, it's not a scary monster. You can even help me tell it to go away. (Practice lifting a forefinger and wagging it at the book while saying "Go away!" Lifting your finger to point will give the toddlers prompts for replying at appropriate times throughout the book.)

Read the Book

Encourage everyone to participate in saying "Go away!"

While reading, pause to briefly discuss concepts or words that may be unfamiliar to toddlers.

Deliver 6 by 6 Message to Caregivers

Another way to make books fun is to find related activities. Here's a song that's about monsters, but it's funny too, just like the book.

Deliver 6 by 6 Message to All Participants

Now we're going to have even more fun with this book by listening to a song about monsters—but don't worry—it's not scary, either. Everyone get up and dance with me!

Introduce and Play the Song

"We Will Stomp," by Eric Litwin and Michael Levine

Encourage everyone to get up and move in the ways the song suggests.

Transition to the Next Book

So that was our first book, *Go Away, Big Green Monster!* Next, we'll read a book about a house where—shhh!—everyone is sleeping.

Introduce the Book

The Napping House, by Audrey Wood

Point out title, author, and illustrator.

Deliver 6 by 6 Message to All Participants

This is another great book for everyone to participate in reading. As I read this book, help me say "Where—shhh—everyone is sleeping" when it's time. We'll read this at another session when we do the **Talk Talk Talk** skill, which is about building vocabulary. Listen for all those different words for sleeping. (Demonstrate lifting your finger to your lips as a prompt for everyone to say "Where—shhh—everyone is sleeping" with you. Help the group practice a few times.)

Read the Book

Encourage everyone to participate in saying the repeated phrase with you.

While reading, pause to briefly discuss concepts or words that may be unfamiliar to toddlers.

Review the Book

In the Napping House, how many were in the bed? Will you count with me? (Open to the spread with everyone on the bed and count the people and animals.) Let's do a rhyme about six in the bed.

Lead the Group in the Action Rhyme

"Six in the Bed," abbreviated from the traditional "Ten in the Bed"

Transition to the Next Book

So that was our second book, about the Napping House, where now, no one is sleeping. Next, we'll read a book about a chick who is stuck in the mud—or is he?

Introduce the Book

Stuck in the Mud, by Jane Clarke

Deliver 6 by 6 Message to All Participants

Here's another book you can help me read. When I say "pushed and pulled again and again," do the motions with me. (Practice lifting hands and making pushing and pulling motions.)

Read the Book

Encourage everyone to participate in doing the actions with you. While reading, pause to briefly discuss concepts or words that may be unfamiliar to toddlers.

Transition to the Closing Song

So that was our third book, *Stuck in the Mud*, by Jane Clarke. Can you remember all three books we read today? (Go over the titles again, in order.) Our third book was our last book for today. So we'll sing our good-bye song, and I'll see you next time!

Sing the Closing Song

"Storytime Is Over" (Tune: "If You're Happy and You Know It")

> Now storytime is over, wave good-bye.
> Now storytime is over, wave good-bye.
> Now storytime is done and I hope you had lots of fun,
> Our storytime is over, wave good-bye.

Invite Participants to Extend Storytime

Let people know they are welcome to come over to see the instrument you use for the call, or to see today's puppet. Invite them to stay and explore your library's children's area.

Have Fun With Books: A Storytime for Pre-Readers

This plan is appropriate for children ages three to five years with a caregiver.
  Materials you will need for this storytime:

- Music and Songs:
  o "Everybody Come and Take" (Tune: "Shortnin' Bread")
  o "If You're Happy and You Know It"
  o "The Cats Go Climbing" (Tune: "When Johnny Comes Marching Home")
  o "I Know an Old Lady Who Swallowed a Fly"
  o "Storytime Is Over" (Tune: "If You're Happy and You Know It")
- Action Rhymes:
  o "Five Little Kittens"
  o "This Is a Melon"
  o "Five Little Monkeys Jumping on the Bed"

- Books:
  - ○ *There Are Cats In This Book*, by Viviane Schwarz
  - ○ *The Watermelon Seed*, by Greg Pizzoli
  - ○ *Bark, George*, by Jules Feiffer

Call Everyone to Storytime

Use a rain stick or other simple instrument to gather everyone's attention, saying something like "Do you hear that? It's the sound of storytime. Time for storytime!" Once everyone is settled in place, introduce yourself and welcome everyone.

Sing the Welcome Song

"Everybody Come and Take" (Tune: "Shortnin' Bread")

> Everybody come and take
> Everybody come and take
> Everybody come and take a seat on the floor.
> Not on the ceiling,
> Not on the door,
> Everybody come and take a seat on the floor.

Sing the Opening Song

Sing a few verses of "If You're Happy and You Know It"
  Conclude with these lyrics:

> Now storytime is starting sit real still,
> Now storytime is starting sit real still,
> Your hands are in your lap, you are sitting down real flat,
> Storytime is starting sit real still.

Give Opening 6 by 6 Message to Caregivers

Today is all about having fun. We want you and your child to enjoy books, reading, and the library. The absolute best way to show the pleasures of reading is to share great books like those in today's storytime.

Introduce and Read the Book

There Are Cats In This Book, by Viviane Schwarz

Lead the Action Rhyme

"Five Little Kittens"

> Five little kittens, standing in a row, (hand in front, all fingers extended)
> The bow their heads to each other so. (bend fingers down then extend back up)
> They run to the left (move hand to the left)
> They run to the right (move hand to the right)
> They stand up and stretch in the bring sunlight. (stretch arm high above head)
> Along comes a dog who's looking for some fun (bring other hand near,
>   pretending to be a dog)
> WOOF WOOF WOOF! Watch those kitty cats run! (quickly hide hand behind
>   back)

Play or Sing the Song

"The Cats Go Climbing" (Tune: "When Johnny Comes Marching Home")

> The cats go climbing one by one. Meow, meow!
> The cats go climbing one by one. Meow, meow!
> The cats go climbing one by one, they will not stop until they're done.
> And they all go climbing up, in the tree, where they hide, in the leaves.
> *Repeat with twos and threes:*
> The cats go climbing two by two, they won't come down, what will I do?
> The cats go climbing three by three, I can't see them, but they see me.

Deliver 6 by 6 Message to Caregivers

Kids who are curious about books will naturally want to learn to read. We can help you find books on topics your child is interested in or books that have situations kids find familiar. Almost every child can relate to this poor alligator in this next story, which makes it perfect for our **Have Fun With Books** storytime.

Introduce and Read the Book

The Watermelon Seed by Greg Pizzoli
    Point out title, author, and illustrator.

Lead the Action Rhyme

"This Is a Melon"

This is a melon. (make small, open circle by touching tip of thumb and index
   finger on one hand)
This is a melon. (make a larger, open circle by touching fingertips together of
   both hands)
A great big melon I see! (make a very large, open circle with hands above head)
Are you ready?
Can you count them?
One, two, three! (make three circles again as you count smallest to largest)

Play or Sing the Song

"I Know an Old Lady Who Swallowed a Fly"

Deliver 6 by 6 Message to Caregivers

It's important that you read a little bit together every single day, but don't force
it. If we (and I mean all adults) help kids understand that reading can be enjoyable and avoid making it feel like a punishment or chore, they will be more
motivated to learn to read on their own.

Lead the Action Rhyme

"Five Little Monkeys Jumping on the Bed"

Introduce and Read the Book

Bark, George, by Jules Feiffer

Sing the Closing Song

"Storytime Is Over" (Tune: "If You're Happy and You Know It")

   Now storytime is over, wave good-bye.
   Now storytime is over, wave good-bye.
   Now storytime is done and I hope you had lots of fun,
   Our storytime is over, wave good-bye.

Invite Participants to Extend Storytime

Invite them to stay and explore your library's children's area.

HAVE FUN WITH BOOKS: A REPRODUCIBLE STORYTIME GUIDE FOR EARLY TALKERS

Call Everyone to Storytime

Give Opening 6 by 6 Message to Caregivers

Today is all about having fun. We want you and your child to enjoy reading books together and equate that book sharing time with love and affection. Your baby's brain is developing rapidly in these first few years so it's the perfect time to tell stories, sing, talk about pictures, and play. I am so happy you brought your baby to storytime today!

Sing the Welcome Song
"Peek-a-Boo"

Sing the Opening Song
"This Is the Way We Wave Hello"

Introduce the Book
Moo, Baa, La La La!, by Sandra Boynton

Deliver 6 by 6 Message to Caregivers

Even though this book is a little small to share in a group like this one, I am hopeful you can see how much fun it would be to share one-on-one. If not already, your child will soon be able to focus on the pictures. When that happens, you can pause and spend more time looking at and talking about the ones that seem to interest her the most.

Lead the Action Rhyme
"Tick Tock"

Introduce and Play the Song
"Touch Your Toes," from *Diaper Gym*

Introduce and Play the Song
"My Little Hands," from *Diaper Gym*

Introduce the Book
Pajama Time!, by Sandra Boynton

Deliver 6 by 6 Message to Caregivers

I mentioned earlier how quickly your baby's brain is developing. The whole chemistry of the brain changes when your baby (or anyone, for that matter!) is in a comfortable and happy environment. The serotonin released in the body helps the brain more easily retain those experiences and use them as the foundation for later learning.

Lead the Action Rhyme
"Tummy Button"

Deliver 6 by 6 Message to All Participants

We are nearing the end of our storytime, so it's time for our final story and rhyme. I hope you will check out a few books to take home and find a bit of time every day to read together. If your baby gets fussy and doesn't want to stay calm, don't feel bad about putting the book down and trying again later. It doesn't have to be one long stretch of time, either. Just a few minutes here and there will help babies learn to love books.

Introduce the Book and Song

Brown Bear, Brown Bear, What Do You See?, by Bill Martin Jr. and "Brown Bear, Brown Bear, What Do You See?" from *Playing Favorites*, by Greg and Steve

Lead the Action Rhyme
"Criss Cross Applesauce"

From *Six Skills by Age Six: Launching Early Literacy at the Library* by Anna Foote and Bradley Debrick.
Santa Barbara, CA: Libraries Unlimited. Copyright © 2016.

HAVE FUN WITH BOOKS: A REPRODUCIBLE STORYTIME GUIDE FOR TALKERS

Call Everyone to Storytime

Give Opening 6 by 6 Message to Caregivers

Today's early literacy skill is **Have Fun With Books**. Children who enjoy books and reading will want to learn to read when it's time. Storytime is all about having fun with books, and during this session we'll talk about some ways to enhance the fun you can have with books whenever and wherever you read. We'll also preview some books that we'll use in future sessions when we feature the other skills.

Sing or Play the Welcome Song
"The More We Get Together," traditional.

Introduce the Puppet
Show the mouse puppet. Say that there will be a mouse in one of today's stories and that we will start with a poem about a mouse. Use the puppet to help illustrate the rhyme as you recite it.

Read/Recite the Poem
"Hickory Dickory Dock," traditional.

Introduce the Book
Go Away, Big Green Monster!, by Ed Emberley

Deliver 6 by 6 Message to Caregivers

One way to show children books are fun is to have them participate in reading with you. As I read this book, I'll have you all help me say "Go away!" when it's time.

Deliver 6 by 6 Message to All Participants

In this story, a monster will appear. But don't worry, it's not a scary monster. You can even help me tell it to go away. (Practice lifting a forefinger and wagging it at the book while saying "Go away!" Lifting your finger to point will give the toddlers prompts for replying at appropriate times throughout the book.)

Read the Book

Deliver 6 by 6 Message to Caregivers

Another way to make books fun is to find related activities. Here's a song that's about monsters, but it's funny too, just like the book.

Deliver 6 by 6 Message to All Participants

Now we're going to have even more fun with this book by listening to a song about monsters—but don't worry—it's not scary, either. Everyone get up and dance with me!

Introduce and Play the Song
"We Will Stomp," by Eric Litwin and Michael Levine

Introduce the Book
The Napping House, by Audrey Wood

Deliver 6 by 6 Message to All Participants ·

This is another great book for everyone to participate in reading. As I read this book, help me say "Where—shhh—everyone is sleeping" when it's time. We'll read this at another session when we do the **Talk Talk Talk** skill, which is about building vocabulary. Listen for all those different words for sleeping. (Demonstrate lifting your finger to your lips as a prompt for everyone to say "Where—shhh—everyone is sleeping" with you. Help the group practice a few times.)

Read the Book

Lead the Group in the Action Rhyme
"Six in the Bed," abbreviated from the traditional "Ten in the Bed"

Introduce the Book
Stuck in the Mud, by Jane Clarke

Deliver 6 by 6 Message to All Participants

Here's another book you can help me read. When I say "pushed and pulled again and again," do the motions with me. (Practice lifting hands and making pushing and pulling motions.)

Read the Book

Sing the Closing Song
"Storytime Is Over" (Tune: "If You're Happy and You Know It")

From *Six Skills by Age Six: Launching Early Literacy at the Library* by Anna Foote and Bradley Debrick.
Santa Barbara, CA: Libraries Unlimited. Copyright © 2016.

HAVE FUN WITH BOOKS: A REPRODUCIBLE STORYTIME GUIDE FOR PRE-READERS

Call Everyone to Storytime

Sing the Welcome Song
"Everybody Come and Take" (Tune: "Shortnin' Bread")

Sing the Opening Song
"If You're Happy and You Know It"

Give Opening 6 by 6 Message to Caregivers

Today is all about having fun. We want you and your child to enjoy books, reading, and the library. The absolute best way to show the pleasures of reading is to share great books like those in today's storytime.

Introduce and Read the Book
There Are Cats In This Book, by Viviane Schwarz

Lead the Action Rhyme
"Five Little Kittens"

Play or Sing the Song
"The Cats Go Climbing" (Tune: "When Johnny Comes Marching Home")

Deliver 6 by 6 Message to Caregivers

Kids who are curious about books will naturally want to learn to read. We can help you find books on topics your child is interested in or books that have situations kids find familiar. Almost every child can relate to this poor alligator in this next story which makes it perfect for our **Have Fun With Books** storytime.

Introduce and Read the Book
The Watermelon Seed, by Greg Pizzoli

Lead the Action Rhyme
"This Is a Melon"

Play or Sing the Song
"I Know an Old Lady Who Swallowed a Fly"

Deliver 6 by 6 Message to Caregivers

It's important that you read a little bit together every single day, but don't force it. If we (and I mean all adults) help kids understand that reading can be enjoyable and avoid making it feel like a punishment or chore, they will be more motivated to learn to read on their own.

Lead the Action Rhyme
"Five Little Monkeys Jumping on the Bed"

Introduce and Read the Book
Bark, George, by Jules Feiffer

Sing the Closing Song
"Storytime Is Over" (Tune: "If You're Happy and You Know It")

Looking Ahead

Have Fun With Books is one of the six key skills children need to have experienced by about age six to be ready to learn to read. Though it is the first skill we address in this book, we'd like to point out that we can foster all of these skills in children simultaneously as we read, sing, and play with them—starting from the day they are born. However, we did choose to begin with this skill because without an understanding of the importance—and potential joy—of reading, many children lack the desire to do the hard work of learning to read. Instilling a love of reading and learning from an early age is one of the finest gifts we can give children.

In our next chapter, we'll look at another of the six skills, **Talk Talk Talk**.

References

Barnett, Mac. *Sam & Dave Dig a Hole*. Somerville, MA: Candlewick, 2014.

Beall, Pamela Conn and Susan Hagen Nipp. *Wee Sing for Baby*. New York: Price Stern Sloan, an imprint of Penguin Young Readers Group, 2002. Used with permission.

Boynton, Sandra. *Moo, Baa, La La La!*. New York: Little Simon, 1995.

Boynton, Sandra. *Pajama Time!*. New York: Workman, 2000.

Clarke, Jane. *Stuck in the Mud*. New York: Walker, 2008.

Corbett, Pie. *The Kingfisher Playtime Treasury: A Collection of Playground Rhymes, Games, and Action Songs*. London: Kingfisher Books, 1989. Used with permission.

Dobbins, Jan. *Driving My Tractor*. Cambridge, MA.: Barefoot Books, 2009.

Emberley, Ed. *Go Away, Big Green Monster!*. Boston: Little, Brown, 1992.

Feiffer, Jules. *Bark, George*. New York: HarperCollins, 1999.

Franceschelli, Christopher. *Alphablock*. New York: Abrams Appleseed, 2013.

Gibbs, Edward. *I Spy on the Farm*. Somerville, MA: Templar Books, 2013.

Hulbert, Laura. *Who Has These Feet?*. New York: H. Holt, 2011.

Jenkins, Steve. *Actual Size*. Boston: Houghton Mifflin, 2004.

Lewis, Kevin. *Chugga-Chugga Choo-Choo*. New York: Scholastic, 1999.

Litwin, Eric. *Pete the Cat: I Love My White Shoes*. New York: Harper, 2010.

Martin, Bill, Jr. *Brown Bear, Brown Bear, What Do You See?*. New York: H. Holt, 1992.

Pizzoli, Greg. *The Watermelon Seed*. New York: Disney Hyperion, 2013.

Rosenthal, Amy Krouse. *Little Pea*. San Franciso: Chronicle Books, 2005.

Rueda, Claudia. *Huff & Puff: Can You Blow Down the Houses of the Three Little Pigs?*. New York: Abrams Appleseed, 2012.

Schwartz, David M., and Yael Schy. *Where in the Wild?: Camouflaged Creatures Concealed . . . and Revealed*. Berkeley, CA: Tricycle, 2007.

Schwarz, Viviane. *There Are Cats in This Book*. Cambridge, MA: Candlewick, 2008.

Shannon, David. *Duck on a Bike*. New York: Blue Sky, 2002.

Tullet, Hervé. *Press Here*. San Francisco: Chronicle Books, 2011.

Wood, Audrey. *The Napping House*. San Diego: Harcourt Brace Jovanovich, 1984.

Chapter 5

Talk Talk Talk

Talk Talk Talk means children learn the names of things concepts and ideas; this is the concept of "vocabulary" in the early literacy field. Learning vocabulary is important because the more words children know, the easier it is for them to recognize words once they begin to sound them out on their own. A child who has never heard the word "pantry," for example, will have a much harder time moving from "pan" plus "try" to "pantry" than a child who knows that a pantry is a cupboard in the kitchen.

Interaction: A Key to Learning This Skill

The landmark study by Betty Hart and Todd R. Risley published in the book *Meaningful Differences in the Everyday Experience of Young American Children* found that the overall number of words young children hear makes a difference in the size of the cumulative vocabularies at age three. The difference is so great that the phrase "30 million word gap" arose from this research. Adults who talk to children throughout the day are giving them a great advantage when it comes to learning vocabulary and becoming ready to learn to read.

The good news is that anyone can make a conscious effort to speak more with children—this is one of the messages we love sharing with parents and caregivers. You can advise them that one easy way to start speaking more is to narrate the day, telling children what they are doing while they are doing it and asking children to do the same.

As children age, they are able to learn increasingly complex vocabulary. Let's start with an example. One of the best ways to help children build vocabulary is to enrich the statements they make. If you hold up a blue ball and ask a toddler what it is, you might hear "ball" or "a ball." An enriching response to this would be, "Yes, it is a ball, a round, blue ball. It will be fun to play with." Babies begin by learning the names of concrete things they can see (ball), toddlers begin to learn concepts (round and blue), and by preschool age, most children are ready to learn the names of ideas (fun).

And of course, a favorite way for parents as well as librarians to interact with children is by using picture books. This experience also provides an opportunity to expand children's vocabularies. One study found that picture books contain seven times more rare words than everyday conversation, and hearing unusual words gives children a chance to learn their meanings. Since picture books aim at telling a complete story in a very compact way, authors choose the best words to tell their stories, resulting in texts rich in rare words.

Activities That Help Children Develop This Skill

- Talk to children as much as possible. Hearing many different words is important, but so is the total number of words children hear while they are young.

- Narrate children's and your activities as you go through the day. This allows children to hear many words.
- While reading, don't skip over unfamiliar words or substitute easier words for difficult ones. Preview unfamiliar words if you are concerned about stopping the flow of the story to discuss new words.
- Point out objects (in books and all around) that are unfamiliar to children. Name them and discuss their purposes.
- Find real-world versions of items you see while reading.
- Have children describe the illustrations in books and enrich their descriptions. If the child says, "That's a ball," say, "Right, that's a blue ball. It's big, too! It would be fun to play with." Young children learn the names of things they can see (ball); as children age, they learn the names of concepts and ideas (blue, big, fun). By adding on to children's sentences, we can help them move along in that process.
- Attach labels to items in the room such as "door" and "window." This helps with **Talk Talk Talk** and also with **Notice Print All Around You**.
- Name not just objects but actions, ideas, feelings, and other abstract concepts.

Books That Are Very Good for Talk Talk Talk

Note: Most high-quality picture books will illustrate more than one skill. These just happen to be some of our favorites to help children learn this skill.

Big Little, by Leslie Patricelli
Comparing and contrasting is an excellent way to build vocabulary. This book features pairs of things kids will recognize, and states that one is big and the other is little. It's a fantastic springboard to talk about other things that are big and little in the child's natural world.

The Black Rabbit, by Philippa Leathers
Rabbit is frightened! A large black rabbit is following him everywhere he goes, and Rabbit can't elude the pursuer. Bewildered and desperate, he runs into the deep, dark wood only to find an even more terrifying villain ready to chase him back out again. With surprises for Rabbit at every turn, this story of light and dark will leave preschoolers feeling very clever as they figure out what's really going on.

Brown Bear, Brown Bear, What Do You See?, by Bill Martin Jr.
The large, colorful animals drawn by Eric Carle can be used as a springboard for further discussion. Where does a bear live? What does a duck eat? When was the last time you saw a horse? Pair this book with a simple nonfiction title about one of the featured animals and you've got a **Talk Talk Talk** powerhouse.

The Chicken Thief, by Béatrice Rodriguez
Oh dear! Fox has stolen Hen and run off with her. Will Bear, Rabbit, and Rooster be able to rescue Hen? And does she need to be rescued? Fox, though sly, may just have good intentions for Hen. This wordless book's hilarious illustrations

are bound to spark a wealth of conversation. Be sure to take a look at the other books in this series to see whether Fox and Hen are able to live happily ever after.

Click, Clack, Moo: Cows That Type, by Doreen Cronin
Farmer Brown's cows are cold at night in the barn, so they type him a note to demand electric blankets and go on a "no milk" strike until their demands are met. What will Farmer have to do to keep peace on his farm? This silly story is perfect for working on noticing print since it features the act of writing and is illustrated with various fonts. It is also rich in vocabulary words ("impossible" and "typewriter," for example) and phrases ("on strike" and "neutral party").

Digger, Dozer, Dumper, by Hope Vestergaard
"Trucks that sweep and dig and shift./Trucks that dump and tow and lift." From street sweeper to excavator to cherry picker, this book offers engaging rhyming poems about 16 different machines. This one is great for building vocabulary—in addition to listing the names of various machines, there are plenty of complementary words like "asphalt," "rig," and "cargo." Good for reading a poem at a time, though some readers will want to devour the book in one sitting. Extend the fun by exploring the book's final question, "Which truck would YOU like to be?"

Dinosaur Roar!, by Paul and Henrietta Stickland
Rhyming couplets present all kinds of dinosaurs and their behaviors: "Dinosaur roar, dinosaur squeak/dinosaur fierce, dinosaur meek . . ." Help children learn the **Look for Letters** skill by exploring the idea of opposites presented in the book, and help them learn vocabulary by talking about some of the unusual words—just what does "meek" mean, anyway? The high-interest subject and bright, large illustrations make this a good group storytime book.

Duck! Rabbit!, by Amy Krouse Rosenthal and Tom Lichtenheld
Is it a duck? Or a rabbit? Two unseen narrators argue over whether the story's strange character is a duck or a rabbit. One is sure the odd animal is acting like a duck; the other is positive it's behaving like a rabbit. This book invites interaction and debate, leaving readers with plenty to compare, contrast, and discuss.

Go Away, Big Green Monster!, by Ed Emberley
This classic book uses die-cut pages to make a monster's face appear and then disappear, feature by feature. Children feel empowered to tell the monster to "Go away!" one feature at time. Exploring the names of facial features builds vocabulary for young children and the die-cuts make for fun discussion of the shapes you can see in this book. This is a wonderful story for retelling by using a puppet, felt board, or pieces of paper. Be sure to check out Emberley's companion title, *Nighty Night, Little Green Monster*.

Good Night, Gorilla, by Peggy Rathmann
In this classic, nearly wordless picture book, a zookeeper thinks he's putting all the animals to bed, but a mischievous gorilla follows behind him, letting all the animals out. Everyone follows Zookeeper home to bed, and it's left to his surprised wife to get all the animals back to the zoo. Because it relies heavily on illustration, this book allows even very young children to retell the story, even after just one pass through.

Hide and Seek Harry around the House, by Kenny Harrison
It's easy to **Talk Talk Talk** about all the household items behind which Harry the hippopotamus is trying to hide. Encourage parents to use this book one page at a time—even without the text—and just explore the vocabulary of the uncluttered images.

How To Be a Cat, by Nikki McClure
Big Cat is there to guide Kitten as she learns to stretch, stalk, pounce, and do all the things that cats do. Point out the word that describes the action Kitten is doing (it's fun to have kids mimic the actions, too!). Tell the story from the pictures, and add lots of your own descriptive words. This expands vocabulary and helps with comprehension.

LMNO Peas, by Keith Baker
This imaginative alphabet book features peas as the main characters, and lists and shows lots of their occupations. Take the B page for example, "B: We're builders, bathers, and bikers in a race." Readers will get a kick out of exploring the funny illustrations of peas driving cars, playing a saxophone, and parachuting from the sky (to name a few). Great for **Look for Letters** and **Talk Talk Talk**.

Meeow and the Little Chairs, by Sebastien Braun
Meeow, a black cat, has his friends Baa, Moo, Quack, and Woof over to play. They line up different colors of chairs; Meeow rings a bell, and Moo blows his whistle. "What can they be doing? Ding-ding! Choo-choo!" They have made a train. The simple story line and bold illustrations make this a good choice for baby and toddler storytimes. Learning the concept of colors makes this a good book for **Talk Talk Talk**. Exploring the sounds like "ding" and "choo" will help young children learn and express the **Take Time to Rhyme, Sing and Play Word Games** skill. After reading, act out the story using chairs or pillows to reinforce the **Tell Stories** skill for children.

Nana in the City, by Lauren Castillo
A young boy is frightened of the busy, noisy city until his Nana makes him a special gift that allows him to see the city in a different light. Develop the **Talk Talk Talk** skill by discussing the new and unusual words the boy encounters in the city-specific scenes. In addition to what the boy sees, also talk about what he might be feeling. Intangible concepts like emotions are often difficult for

children to verbalize. This book is a perfect avenue for developing that specific vocabulary.

The Napping House, by Audrey Wood
A classic cumulative tale in which nearly everyone is asleep . . . for a while at least. An abundance of rich words are placed carefully in this story: dozing, snoozing, dreaming, slumbering. The story's structure lets you hear those words over and over as you read. Try using some of these rare words in the daily conversations with children. This is a great title to have children read along with you, prompting them to repeat the phrase, "where everyone is sleeping." And because of the sharp contrast of the weather at the beginning and the end of this book, it's a great one to retell using three two-page spreads, one each from the beginning, middle, and end.

One Big Building: A Counting Book about Construction, by Michael Dahl
This book uses construction machines to illustrate the concept of counting from 1 to 12. The book's design gives readers plenty of opportunity to explore counting. The pages are numbered, and each page features the word (for example, "three"), the numeral ("3"), and the appropriate number of dots for counting. And each number page lists and illustrates a correct number of machines ("THREE dump trucks haul away the dirt."). Seeing all of the different ways to express number concepts will help children develop the **Notice Print** skill. Talking about different ways of expressing the same idea ("three") also helps children learn the **Look for Letters** skill, because knowing "same" versus "different" is an important step in developing letter recognition skills. Older children will be able to distinguish between numbers and letters.

Peck, Peck, Peck, by Lucy Cousins
Today's the day baby woodpecker learns to peck from his daddy. And once he learns, he can't seem to stop! This overzealous bird gets into the house and pecks everything he finds, including "an eggplant, a tangerine, a butter dish, a nectarine, a green bean, a sardine, and seventeen jelly beans." The unusual words and rhymes make this good for young children to learn and explore the **Talk Talk Talk** and **Take Time to Rhyme** skills.

Pepi Sings a New Song, by Laura Ljungkvist
Pepi is a curious bird with a knack for learning new words. He travels from place to place absorbing all kinds of location-specific vocabulary. This is a fiction book, but it has a nonfiction feel almost like a visual dictionary. There are many things to **Talk Talk Talk** about and look for in daily life.

Pomelo's Opposites, by Ramona Badescu
An adorably stylized elephant explores the ins and outs and ups and downs of opposites. Don't let the cutesy nature of this book fool you; it's a true marvel for sharing with **Pre-Readers**. Some opposite pairs are ordinary, but some are unusual.

These unusual words and concepts will likely inspire conversations that will in turn enrich everyone's vocabulary.

Same Same, by Marthe Jocelyn
Three images on each two-page spread share one common bond. The author tells you only what the objects have in common; she doesn't tell you what the objects are. The same illustration could be the earth, a globe, a planet, or a ball. Start with the word your child knows (or thought of first) and expand their vocabulary with other options. There are no right or wrong answers, so success is guaranteed.

Tuck Me In!, by Dean Hacohen
Time for bed, baby animals! Who needs to be tucked in? One by one, Baby Pig, Baby Zebra, Baby Moose, and others reply "I do!," and readers then turn half-page "blankets" over the babies in their beds. Pointing out how the half pages are unusual will help children learn the ways books work, and the unusual animals featured will help build their vocabularies.

Who Has These Feet?, by Laura Hulbert
Throughout the book, two-page spreads ask "Who has these feet?" with an illustration of animal feet. The following spread provides the answer in text and picture, along with a simple fact about that animal's feet; for example, "A tree frog has sticky pads on its toes so it can stick to leaves." Readers will have fun guessing which animal has which feet, and the mix of animals featured will help children build vocabulary and background knowledge.

See the last few pages of this chapter for storytime plans for babies, toddlers, and preschoolers that use some of these books.

Connecting the Skills

As mentioned earlier in this chapter, children encounter a significantly higher number of rare words in books than they do in ordinary conversation. Combine **Talk Talk Talk** with **Have Fun With Books** by helping caregivers find books on topics their child is interested in: garbage trucks, horses, volcanoes, or wild animals, to name a few. Don't overlook the high-quality nonfiction that is being published for young children. Those books contain a set of subject-specific vocabulary that is unlikely to be heard anywhere else during their regular routines. Additionally, many nonfiction books employ unexpected page layouts, text blocks, sidebars, and infographics that support the **Notice Print** skill. Just because the text looks different doesn't mean it's not equally as important.

There is also a natural connection between this skill and **Tell Stories About Everything**. Wordless books and old-fashioned storytelling allow the reader/teller to use his or her own personal vocabulary to convey the story. As kids "read" a wordless book, they benefit from the story sequence (**Tell Stories**) and the opportunity to use words they know without the fear of reading one incorrectly. Wordless books are especially wonderful tools for dual-language families or for families who do not speak English at home.

Links to Lifelong Learning

As one of the comprehension skills, **Talk Talk Talk** should not be viewed as one that will ever be mastered. Even as adults, we should continually add words to our own vocabularies whether they be job specific or simply unfamiliar words we read in a book. We should encourage kids to do the same. Encourage them to ask questions when they encounter new words, and help them learn to use those words correctly and confidently. Communication is a highly valued competency in the workplace, and one that is difficult for employers to teach. A rich vocabulary and the self-assurance to use it properly is a trait that will be rewarded time and time again.

Storytime Plans for Talk Talk Talk

The following section includes storytime plans for three age groups:

- **Early Talkers** (birth to approximately 18 months)
- **Talkers** (approximately 18 months to three years)
- **Pre-Readers** (approximately ages three to five years)

Feel free to adapt these plans to make them your own!

Talk Talk Talk: A Storytime for Early Talkers

This plan is appropriate for children birth to 18 months old with a caregiver.
   Materials you will need for this storytime:

- Music and Songs:
  - "Peek-a-Boo" (Tune: "Frère Jacques")
  - "Touch Your Toes" from *Diaper Gym*, by Priscilla Hegner and Rose Grasselli
  - "My Little Hands" from *Diaper Gym*, by Priscilla Hegner and Rose Grasselli
  - "This Is the Way We Wave Hello" (Tune: "Here We Go 'Round the Mulberry Bush")
  - "Brown Bear, Brown Bear, What Do You See?" from *Playing Favorites*, by Greg and Steve

- Action Rhymes:
  - "Round and Round the Garden"
  - "This is Big"
  - "Criss Cross Applesauce" from *The Kingfisher Playtime Treasury*, by Pie Corbett
- Books:
  - *Hide and Seek Harry around the House*, by Kenny Harrison
  - *Big Little*, by Leslie Patricelli
  - *Brown Bear, Brown Bear, What Do You See?*, by Bill Martin Jr.

Call Everyone to Storytime

Use a rain stick or other simple instrument to gather everyone's attention, saying something like "Do you hear that? It's the sound of storytime. Time for storytime!" Once everyone is settled in place, introduce yourself and welcome everyone.

Give Opening 6 by 6 Message to Caregivers

It is easier for new readers to figure out words in print if they already know what the word means. By sharing a lot of words with your baby, you are helping to develop a deep, rich vocabulary that will actually make it easier for her to learn to read.

Sing the Welcome Songs

"Peek-a-Boo" (Tune: "Frère Jacques")

> Peek a boo! Peek a boo!
> I see you! I see you!
> I'm so glad to see you! I'm so glad to see you!
> Peek a boo! Peek a boo!

"This Is the Way We Wave Hello" (Tune: "Here We Go 'Round the Mulberry Bush")

> This is the way we wave hello,
> Wave hello, wave hello.
> This is the way we wave hello
> So early in the morning!

Repeat with other actions such as clap our hands, touch our nose, tap our feet. Finish with wave hello once again.

Deliver 6 by 6 Message to Caregivers

You've probably noticed that we sing "This Is the Way We Wave Hello" every week in storytime. Not only does it set the mood for storytime, but it also reinforces the names of body parts—hands, nose, feet. Kids typically learn the names of important and familiar objects first like body parts, toys, and objects in their environment. This next book has very simple illustrations, so you can talk about all the objects on each page.

Introduce and Read the Book

Hide and Seek Harry around the House, by Kenny Harrison
   Point out title, author, and illustrator.

Lead the Action Rhyme

"Round and Round the Garden." Begin with baby on lap, facing caregiver.

   Round and round the garden (made circles on baby's open palm)
   Goes the little bear.
   One step, two steps, (hop fingers up baby's arm)
   Tickle you under there! (tickle baby)
   Round and round the garden (made circles on baby's open palm)
   Goes the little mouse.
   One step, two steps, (hop fingers up baby's arm)
   Right into his house! (tickle baby)

Introduce and Play the Song

"Touch Your Toes" from *Diaper Gym*, by Priscilla Hegner and Rose Grasselli

Introduce and Play the Song

"My Little Hands" from *Diaper Gym*, by Priscilla Hegner and Rose Grasselli

Deliver 6 by 6 Message to Caregivers

Success in fourth and fifth grades can be attributed to the number of words a child hears between birth and age three. Sharing books together might be the best way to introduce new and rare words that your child may not hear very often elsewhere.

Introduce and Read the Book

Big Little, by Leslie Patricelli

Lead the Action Rhyme

"This Is Big." Begin with baby on lap, facing caregiver. Gently move baby's hands and head to suit actions.

> This is big big big (hands wide apart, side to side)
> And this is small small small (hands close together, side to side)
> This is short short short (hands close together, up and down)
> And this is tall tall tall (hands wide apart, up and down)
> This is fast fast fast (roll hand and over hand quickly)
> And this is slow slow slow (roll hand over hand slowly)
> This is yes yes yes (nod head)
> And this is no no no (shake head side to side)

Deliver 6 by 6 Message to All Participants

We are nearing the end of our storytime, so it's time for our final story and rhyme. We talked a lot about vocabulary today, and I am hopeful you'll do even more "talk talk talking" to your baby than you already have been! While this storytime focused on vocabulary, talking also reveals natural rhythms and patterns of speech. All of those words and sounds are important as your baby is busy learning about language.

Introduce the Book and Song

Brown Bear, Brown Bear, What Do You See?, by Bill Martin Jr. and "Brown Bear, Brown Bear, What Do You See?" from *Playing Favorites,* by Greg and Steve

This book is great to read aloud but can also be sung to a tune similar to "Baa Baa Black Sheep." We will listed to the song while I turn the pages.

Lead the Action Rhyme

"Criss Cross Applesauce." Begin with baby on lap, facing away from caregiver.

> Criss cross applesauce (use finger to make X on baby's back)
> Spiders crawling up your spine (crawl fingers up baby's spine)
> Cool breeze (blow on baby's neck)
> Tight squeeze (hug baby)
> Makes you get the sillies! (tickle baby)

Invite Participants to Extend Storytime

Invite them to stay and explore your library's children's area.

Talk Talk Talk: A Storytime for Talkers

This plan is appropriate for children approximately 18 months to three years old. Materials you will need for this storytime:

- Music and Songs:
  - Rain stick or other simple instrument
  - "The More We Get Together" (sing or find a recorded version, such as Laurie Berkner's on the album *Buzz Buzz.*)
  - "Walk Around," by Dino O'Dell from the album *Itty Bitty Monsters*
  - "Storytime Is Over" (Tune: "If You're Happy and You Know It")
- Puppet:
  - Small mouse
- Poem:
  - "Hickory Dickory Dock," traditional.
- Books:
  - *Meeow and the Little Chairs*, by Sebastien Braun
  - *The Napping House*, by Audrey Wood
  - *Tuck Me In!*, by Dean Hacohen

Call Everyone to Storytime

Use a rain stick or other simple instrument to gather everyone's attention, saying something like "Do you hear that? It's the sound of storytime. Time for storytime!" Once everyone is settled in place, introduce yourself and welcome everyone.

Give Opening 6 by 6 Message to Caregivers

Today's **6 by 6** skill is **Talk Talk Talk**, so it's all about building vocabulary, which means knowing the names of things, concepts, and ideas. Very young children start by learning the names of things they can see, but with toddlers, they are beginning to learn the names of concepts like the color blue, or the spatial concepts of "on" and "in."

Sing or Play the Welcome Song

"The More We Get Together," traditional.

Note: Many adults are familiar with this song. If you use Laurie Berkner's recording and are not going to post all of the lyrics, be sure to make a poster with the names that Laurie sings in her version, so adults can continue to sing along.

Introduce the Puppet

Show the mouse puppet. Say that there will be a mouse in one of today's stories and that we will start with a poem about a mouse. Use the puppet to help illustrate the rhyme as you recite it.

Read/Recite the Poem

"Hickory Dickory Dock," traditional.

> Hickory dickory dock,
> The mouse ran up the clock,
> The clock struck one,
> The mouse ran down,
> Hickory dickory dock.
> Hickory dickory dock,
> The mouse ran up the clock,
> The clock struck two,
> The mouse said, "Boo!"
> Hickory dickory dock.
> Hickory dickory dock,
> The mouse ran up the clock,
> The clock struck three,
> The mouse said, "Whee!"
> Hickory dickory dock.
> Hickory dickory dock,
> The mouse ran up the clock,
> The clock struck four,
> The mouse said, "No more!"
> Hickory dickory dock.

Introduce the Book

Meeow and the Little Chairs, by Sebastien Braun
    Point out title, author, and illustrator.

Deliver 6 by 6 Message to Caregivers

This book explores the concept of colors in a simple but engaging way. Talking often about colors helps children learn them and gives them additional vocabulary. Once children have mastered the basic colors, expand their vocabulary by talking about as many ways to say colors as possible. For example, shades of blue can be "azure" or "navy."

Deliver 6 by 6 Message to All Participants

In this story, we'll hear about a clever cat and his friends, who play together by putting chairs in a line. What do you think they are making? Let's see!

Read the Book

Pause a couple of times while reading to review the colors on a page and to ask about what the friends could be doing by putting the chairs in a line.

While reading, pause to briefly discuss concepts or words that may be unfamiliar to toddlers.

Transition to the Next Book

So that was our first book, *Meeow and the Little Chairs*, by Sebastien Braun. Next, we'll read a book about a house where—shhh!—everyone is sleeping.

Introduce the Book

The Napping House, by Audrey Wood
    Point out title, author, and illustrator.

Deliver 6 by 6 Message to Caregivers

Grown-ups, research has shown that the more words children hear, the easier it is for them to learn to read when the time comes. This means a couple of things. One, children need to hear lots of different words, and this book has many words for "sleeping." Two, the sheer number of words children hear when they are young matters, too. This book is a little longer than many we read in storytime, so it has more words.

Deliver 6 by 6 Message to All Participants

In this book, we'll hear lots of words that mean "sleeping"—listen for them! As I read this book, help me say "Where—shhh—everyone is sleeping" when it's time. (Demonstrate lifting your finger to your lips as a prompt for everyone to say "Where—shhh—everyone is sleeping" with you. Ask the group to practice a few times.)

Read the Book

Encourage everyone to participate in saying the repeated phrase with you.

While reading, pause to briefly discuss concepts or words that may be unfamiliar to toddlers.

Review the Book

Did you hear all of those words for sleeping? (Open to the spread that has the most words for sleeping and list them.) All of these words mean sleeping! Try to use one or more at naptime or bedtime today. Adults, talking about the story after reading it—or retelling it—reinforces new vocabulary.

Transition to the Next Activity

So that was our second book, *The Napping House*. It had a lot of different words for sleeping. Next, I'm going to play a song that has many different ways to move. Let's listen to it and move in the ways it says!

Introduce and Play the Song

"Walk Around," by Dino O'Dell

Encourage everyone to get up and move in the ways the song suggests.

Transition to the Next Book

Great job, everybody! Let's have a seat and get ready for our next book—it's about lots of baby animals going to bed.

Deliver 6 by 6 Message to Caregivers

Adults, researchers have found that picture books have three times more rare words than everyday conversation. This book features some animals we might not usually think to talk about, which gives children more vocabulary.

Deliver 6 by 6 Message to All Participants

Will you help me read this book? When I say "Who else needs to be tucked in?" you say, "I do!" (Give listeners a visual cue when you say "Who else needs to be tucked in?" like extending your hand forward.)

Read the Book

Tuck Me In!, by Dean Hacohen

Encourage everyone to participate in repeating "I do!" with you.

While reading, pause to briefly discuss concepts or words that may be unfamiliar to toddlers.

Transition to the Closing Song

That was our third book, *Tuck Me In!*, by Dean Hacohen. Can you remember all three books we read today? (Go over the titles again, in order.) The third book was our last book for today. So we'll sing our good-bye song, and I'll see you next time!

Sing the Closing Song

"Storytime Is Over" (Tune: "If You're Happy and You Know It")

> Now storytime is over, wave good-bye.
> Now storytime is over, wave good-bye.
> Now storytime is done and I hope you had lots of fun,
> our storytime is over, wave good-bye.

Invite Participants to Extend Storytime

Let people know they are welcome to come over to see the instrument you use for the call, or to see today's puppet. Invite them to stay and explore your library's children's area.

Talk Talk Talk: A Storytime for Pre-Readers

This plan is appropriate for children ages three to five with a caregiver. Materials you will need for this storytime:

- Music and Songs:
  - "Everybody Come and Take" (Tune: "Shortnin' Bread")
  - "If You're Happy and You Know It"
  - "Head, Shoulders, Knees, and Toes"
  - "Shake Your Sillies Out," by Raffi
  - "Storytime Is Over" (Tune: "If You're Happy and You Know It")
- Action Rhymes:
  - "Hop Like a Rabbit"
  - "Here are Grandma's Glasses"
- Books:
  - *Pepi Sings a New Song*, by Laura Ljungkvist
  - *The Napping House*, by Audrey Wood
  - *How To Be a Cat*, by Nikki McClure

Call Everyone to Storytime

Use a rain stick or other simple instrument to gather everyone's attention, saying something like "Do you hear that? It's the sound of storytime. Time for storytime!" Once everyone is settled in place, introduce yourself and welcome everyone.

Sing the Welcome Song

"Everybody Come and Take" (Tune: "Shortnin' Bread")

> Everybody come and take
> Everybody come and take
> Everybody come and take a seat on the floor.
> Not on the ceiling,
> Not on the door,
> Everybody come and take a seat on the floor.

Sing the Opening Song

Sing a few verses of "If You're Happy and You Know It"
   Conclude with these lyrics:

> Now storytime is starting sit real still,
> Now storytime is starting sit real still,
> Your hands are in your lap, you are sitting down real flat,
> Storytime is starting sit real still.

Give Opening 6 by 6 Message to Caregivers

Children's vocabularies grow as they hear more and more words, and children with large listening and speaking vocabularies have an advantage when learning to read. The books I've selected today all have excellent (and sometimes unusual) vocabulary words. Here's our first one. It has a lot of subject-specific words that you may not hear very often.

Introduce and Read the Book

Pepi Sings a New Song, by Laura Ljungkvist

Sing or Play the Song

"Head, Shoulders, Knees, and Toes"

Transition with a Movement Activity

"Hop Like a Rabbit"

> Can you hop like a rabbit?
> Can you jump like a frog?
> Can you walk like a duck?
> Can you run like a dog?
> Can you fly like a bird?
> Can you swim like a fish?
> Can you turn around,
> Then sit like this?

Introduce and Read the Book

How To Be a Cat, by Nikki McClure

Deliver 6 by 6 Message to Caregivers

That book is so simple, but it works perfectly for this skill because Nikki McClune perfectly matches the illustrations with the words. You see the cats stretching, you sense the motion when they pounce. In this case, seeing the picture and hearing the word can help children better understand the word's meaning.

Play or Sing the Song

"Shake Your Sillies Out," by Raffi

Deliver 6 by 6 Message to Caregivers

There are three times as many unusual words in books than there are in normal conversation. When you come across an unfamiliar word, take time to introduce it and explain what it means. You can even start adding some richer words into your regular vocabulary. Instead of saying "I'm tired" you can say "I'm exhausted." Speaking of being tired, our next book uses a lot of different words to describe being asleep.

Introduce and Read the Book

The Napping House, by Audrey Wood

Lead the Action Rhyme

"Here are Grandma's Glasses"

> Here are Grandma's glasses (finger circling eyes like glasses)
> Here is Grandma's hat (hands above head shaping a hat)
> Here is how she folds her hands and put them in her lap. (hands folded in lap)
> Here are Grandma's glasses (finger circling eyes like glasses again)
> Here is Grandma's hat (hands above head shaping a hat again)
> Here is how she folds her hands and takes a little nap. (head resting on folded hands)
> And WOW does she ever snore! (snore loudly!)

Sing the Closing Song

"Storytime Is Over" (Tune: "If You're Happy and You Know It")

> Now storytime is over, wave good-bye.
> Now storytime is over, wave good-bye.
> Now storytime is done and I hope you had lots of fun,
> our storytime is over, wave good-bye.

Invite Participants to Extend Storytime

Invite them to stay and explore your library's children's area.

TALK TALK TALK: A REPRODUCIBLE STORYTIME GUIDE FOR EARLY TALKERS

Call Everyone to Storytime

Give Opening 6 by 6 Message to Caregiver

It is easier for new readers to figure out words in print if they already know what the word means. By sharing a lot of words with your baby, you are helping to develop a deep, rich vocabulary that will actually make it easier for her to learn to read.

Sing the Welcome Songs
"Peek-a-Boo" and "This Is the Way We Wave Hello"

Deliver 6 by 6 Message to Caregivers

You've probably noticed that we sing "This Is the Way We Wave Hello" every week in storytime. Not only does it set the mood for storytime, but it also reinforces the names of body parts—hands, nose, feet. Kids typically learn the names of important and familiar objects first like body parts, toys, and objects in their environment. This next book has very simple illustrations, so you can talk about all the objects on each page.

Introduce and Read the Book
Hide and Seek Harry around the House, by Kenny Harrison

Lead the Action Rhyme
"Round and Round the Garden"

Introduce and Play the Song
"Touch Your Toes" from *Diaper Gym*

Introduce and Play the Song
"My Little Hands" from *Diaper Gym*

Deliver 6 by 6 Message to Caregivers

Success in fourth and fifth grades can be attributed to the number of words a child hears between birth and age three. Sharing books together might be the best way to introduce new and rare words that your child may not hear very often elsewhere.

Introduce and Read the Book
Big Little, by Leslie Patricelli

Lead the Action Rhyme
"This Is Big"

Deliver 6 by 6 Message to All Participants

We are nearing the end of our storytime, so it's time for our final story and rhyme. We talked a lot about vocabulary today, and I am hopeful you'll do even more "talk talk talking" to your baby than you already have been! While this storytime focused on vocabulary, talking also reveals natural rhythms and patterns of speech. All of those words and sounds are important as your baby is busy learning about language.

Introduce the Book and Song
Brown Bear, Brown Bear, What Do You See?, by Bill Martin Jr. and
"Brown Bear, Brown Bear, What Do You See?" from
Playing Favorites, by Greg and Steve

Lead the Action Rhyme
"Criss Cross Applesauce"

TALK TALK TALK: A REPRODUCIBLE STORYTIME GUIDE FOR TALKERS

Call Everyone to Storytime

Give Opening 6 by 6 Message to Caregivers

Today's **6 by 6** skill is **Talk Talk Talk**, so it's all about building vocabulary, which means knowing the names of things, concepts, and ideas. Very young children start by learning the names of things they can see, but with toddlers, they are beginning to learn the names of concepts like the color blue, or the spatial concepts of "on" and "in."

Sing or Play the Welcome Song
"The More We Get Together," traditional.

Introduce the Puppet

Read/Recite the Poem
"Hickory Dickory Dock," traditional.

Introduce the Book
Meeow and the Little Chairs, by Sebastien Braun

Deliver 6 by 6 Message to Caregivers

This book explores the concept of colors in a simple but engaging way. Talking often about colors helps children learn them and gives them additional vocabulary. Once children have mastered the basic colors, expand their vocabulary by talking about as many ways to say colors as possible. For example, shades of blue can be "azure" or "navy."

Deliver 6 by 6 Message to All Participants

In this story, we'll hear about a clever cat and his friends, who play together by putting chairs in a line. What do you think they are making? Let's see!

Read the Book

Introduce the Book
The Napping House, by Audrey Wood

Deliver 6 by 6 Message to Caregivers

Grown-ups, research has shown that the more words children hear, the easier it is for them to learn to read when the time comes. This means a couple of things. One, children need to hear lots of different words, and this book has many words for "sleeping." Two, the sheer number of words children hear when they are young matters, too. This book is a little longer than many we read in storytime, so it has more words.

Deliver 6 by 6 Message to All Participants

In this book, we'll hear lots of words that mean "sleeping"—listen for them! As I read this book, help me say "Where—shhh—everyone is sleeping" when it's time. (Demonstrate lifting your finger to your lips as a prompt for everyone to say "Where—shhh—everyone is sleeping" with you. Ask the group to practice a few times.)

Read the Book

Introduce and Play the Song
"Walk Around," by Dino O'Dell

Introduce the Book
Tuck Me In!, by Dean Hacohen

Deliver 6 by 6 Message to Caregivers

Adults, researchers have found that picture books have three times more rare words than everyday conversation. This book features some animals we might not usually think to talk about, which gives children more vocabulary.

Deliver 6 by 6 Message to All Participants

Will you help me read this book? When I say "Who else needs to be tucked in?" you say, "I do!" (Give listeners a visual cue when you say "Who else needs to be tucked in?" like extending your hand forward.)

Read the Book

Sing the Closing Song
"Storytime Is Over" (Tune: "If You're Happy and You Know It")

TALK TALK TALK: A REPRODUCIBLE STORYTIME GUIDE FOR PRE-READERS

Call Everyone to Storytime

Sing the Welcome Song
"Everybody Come and Take" (Tune: "Shortnin' Bread")

Sing the Opening Song
"If You're Happy and You Know It"

Give Opening 6 by 6 Message to Caregivers

Children's vocabularies grow as they hear more and more words, and children with large listening and speaking vocabularies have an advantage when learning to read. The books I've selected today all have excellent (and sometimes unusual) vocabulary words. Here's our first one. It has a lot of subject-specific words that you may not hear very often.

Introduce and Read the Book
Pepi Sings a New Song, by Laura Ljungkvist

Sing or Play the Song
"Head, Shoulders, Knees, and Toes"

Transition with a Movement Activity
"Can You Stretch?"

Introduce and Read the Book
How To Be a Cat, by Nikki McClure

Deliver 6 by 6 Message to Caregivers

That book is so simple, but it works perfectly for this skill because Nikki McClune perfectly matches the illustrations with the words. You see the cats stretching, you sense the motion when they pounce. In this case, seeing the picture and hearing the word can help a child better understand the word's meaning.

Play or Sing the Song
"Shake Your Sillies Out," by Raffi

Deliver 6 by 6 Message to Caregivers

There are three times as many unusual words in books than there are in normal conversation. When you come across an unfamiliar word, take time to introduce it and explain what it means. You can even start adding some richer words into your regular vocabulary. Instead of saying "I'm tired" you can say "I'm exhausted." Speaking of being tired, our next book uses a lot of different words to describe being asleep.

Introduce and Read the Book
The Napping House, by Audrey Wood

Lead the Action Rhyme
"Here are Grandma's Glasses"

Sing the Closing Song
"Storytime Is Over" (Tune: "If You're Happy and You Know It")

From *Six Skills by Age Six: Launching Early Literacy at the Library* by Anna Foote and Bradley Debrick. Santa Barbara, CA: Libraries Unlimited. Copyright © 2016.

Looking Ahead

Talk Talk Talk is one of the six skills children need to have experienced by about age six to be ready to learn to read. Although it is the second skill we address in this book, children learn all of these skills simultaneously as we read, sing, and play with them. **Talk Talk Talk** is important to children's literacy development because the more words children hear—in sheer number *and* in variety—the better able they are to recognize words when they begin to sound them out.

In our next chapter, we'll explore another of the six skills, **Take Time to Rhyme, Sing and Play Word Games**.

References

Badescu, Ramona. *Pomelo's Opposites*. New York: Enchanted Lion Books, 2013.

Baker, Keith. *LMNO Peas*. New York: Beach Lane Books, 2010.

Braun, Sebastien. *Meeow and the Little Chairs*. London: Boxer Books, 2009.

Castillo, Lauren. *Nana in the City*. New York: Clarion Books, 2014.

Corbett, Pie. *The Kingfisher Playtime Treasury: A Collection of Playground Rhymes, Games, and Action Songs*. London: Kingfisher Books, 1989. Used with permission.

Cousins, Lucy. *Peck, Peck, Peck*. Somerville, MA: Candlewick, 2013.

Cronin, Doreen. *Click, Clack, Moo: Cows That Type*. New York: Simon & Schuster Books for Young Readers, 2000.

Dahl, Michael. *One Big Building: A Counting Book about Construction*. Minneapolis: Picture Window Books, 2004.

Emberley, Ed. *Go Away, Big Green Monster!*. Boston: Little, Brown, 1992.

Hacohen, Dean, and Sherry Scharschmidt. *Tuck Me in!*. Somerville, MA: Candlewick, 2010.

Harrison, Kenny. *Hide and Seek Harry around the House*. Somerville, MA: Candlewick, 2014.

Hart, Betty and Todd R. Risley. *Meaningful Differences in the Everyday Experience of Young American Children*. Baltimore, MD: P.H. Brookes, 1995.

Hulbert, Laura. *Who Has These Feet?*. New York: Henry Holt, 2011.

Jocelyn, Marthe. *Same Same*. Toronto: Tundra Books, 2009.

Leathers, Philippa. *The Black Rabbit*. Somerville, MA: Candlewick, 2013.

Ljungkvist, Laura. *Pepi Sings a New Song*. New York: Beach Lane Books, 2010.

Martin, Bill, Jr. *Brown Bear, Brown Bear, What Do You See?* New York: H. Holt, 1992.

McClure, Nikki. *How To Be a Cat*. New York: Abrams Appleseed, 2013.

Patricelli, Leslie. *Big Little*. Cambridge, MA: Candlewick, 2003.

Rathmann, Peggy. *Good Night, Gorilla*. New York: Putnam, 1994.

Rodriguez, Béatrice. *The Chicken Thief*. Brooklyn: Enchanted Lion Books, 2010.

Rosenthal, Amy Krouse, and Tom Lichtenheld. *Duck! Rabbit!* San Francisco: Chronicle Books, 2009.

Stickland, Paul, and Henrietta Stickland. *Dinosaur Roar!* New York: Dutton Children's Books, 1994.

Vestergaard, Hope. *Digger, Dozer, Dumper.* Somerville, MA: Candlewick, 2013.

Wood, Audrey. *The Napping House.* San Diego: Harcourt Brace Jovanovich, 1984.

Chapter 6

Take Time to Rhyme, Sing and Play Word Games

Take Time to Rhyme, Sing and Play Word Games is called Phonological Awareness in the early literacy field. Basically, it means that children are able to hear the smaller sounds in words, including syllables and phonemes (single sounds like the "buh" the letter B signifies). Children who have experience with this skill are more easily able to sound out words when they are learning to read. As noted in the "pantry" example from the **Talk Talk Talk** chapter, a child who can recognize the syllables "pan" and "try" will have a much easier time sounding out the word than one who cannot.

Play: A Key to Learning This Skill

Play is key to fostering this skill in children—playing with words and their sounds gives children practice in hearing, recognizing, and making the smaller sounds that make up words. There are many good ways to do this.

- Rhyming helps children hear the beginning sounds of words. Because rhyming words end with the same sounds, they highlight the different initial sounds for children.
- Alliteration helps children identify the ending sounds in words, since alliterative words begin with the same sounds. Alliteration also helps **Pre-Readers** begin to match letters to their sounds.
- Singing and listening to music allow children to hear and play with the syllables that make up words. With most lyrics, the notes in the song naturally break words into syllables.
- Word games keep things light and fun, but children are learning all the while. A fun game is changing the first sounds in words to make silly sounds (change the "s" in sip to "b" and you have "bip").

Activities That Help Children Develop This Skill

- Frequently use rhymes, songs, and action rhymes (such as "Open, Shut Them" or "The Itsy-Bitsy Spider").
- Sing, sing, sing—even if you can't carry a tune. Children can't tell that you're off-key, but singing will help them hear the smaller sounds in words.
- Talk about words that rhyme—if the book you're reading has a cat in it, pause to ask "What rhymes with cat?" If the children are too young to answer you, answer your own question—children can hear and understand rhymes before they can say them on their own.
- Talk about words that start with the same sound (alliteration), like "chugga chugga choo choo."
- Make up silly words that sound alike: "Emily Bemily."
- Select a sound of the day and have fun renaming your children's toys with names starting with that sound.

- Help children draw a picture or make a collage of pictures cut from magazines that focus on one sound, like the "kuh" in car, cat, and ketchup. Focus on the sound, not on the name of the letter.
- Use word endings to create as many rhymes as possible. How many words can we make that end with "-at?" Bat, cat, sat, pat, and so on. The words don't even have to make sense, just rhyme!
- Clap out words into their syllables—"monkey" gets two claps, "banana" gets three.
- Play an advanced version of I Spy: "I spy with my little eye something in this room that is round and rhymes with rock . . . "

Books That Are Very Good for Take Time to Rhyme, Sing and Play Word Games

Note: Most high-quality picture books will illustrate more than one skill. These just happen to be some of our favorites to help children learn this skill.

Barnyard Banter, by Denise Fleming
A bouncy, rhyming romp through the barnyard. **Notice Print** as it moves around the page, **Have Fun** looking for the goose that appears on every spread, and of course, **Take Time to Rhyme** with the animal sounds. Read the book slowly and encourage kids to listen to the sounds and complete the rhyme before you do.

Bear Sees Colors, by Karma Wilson
Colors, colors everywhere! Can you find colors just like Bear? Rhyming words give hints to help children predict what color is coming on the next page. When you turn the page, there is a myriad of things to see and talk about. For younger readers, focus on the colors for **Take Time to Rhyme.** For older readers who get the rhymes easily, look at all the details and make this an experience in **Talk Talk Talk.**

Brown Bear, Brown Bear, What Do You See?, by Bill Martin Jr.
One of the quintessential storytime books. The repeating cadence and perfectly composed illustrations help the youngest of readers gain reading confidence. Print motivation achieved! Have children help turn the pages. Singing your way through this book adds another level of fun and helps with **Take Time to Rhyme.** To emphasize **Take Time to Rhyme** for this book, encourage your audience to repeat the phrases "what do you see" and "looking at me" with you.

Bubble Gum, Bubble Gum, by Lisa Wheeler
By the time this story is through, everyone has gum in their feathers and fur. Rhythm and rhyme make this a fantastic read-aloud. Practice ahead of time and you'll start to feel a natural way to split the rhyme at the page turn, encouraging your audience to guess which animal will meet its gooey fate next.

Chugga-Chugga Choo-Choo, by Kevin Lewis
So many children's books rhyme, and this one does, too. But it also features alliteration, meaning that some words begin with the same sound but end differently, like "chugga" and "choo." Alliteration is good for the **Take Time to Rhyme** skill, because it's another way for children to learn to hear the smaller sounds in words. This title is also great for **Have Fun With Books** because children can participate in the story by sounding the train's whistle throughout the book.

Dog's Colorful Day: A Messy Story about Colors and Counting, by Emma Dodd
As Dog goes through his day, he makes messes and attracts colorful spots, and each comes with its own sound. "Splosh! A drop of pink ice cream lands on his right ear" . . . orange juice goes "splurt!". . . a bee drops yellow pollen, "swish!" Playing with these funny words helps children hear the smaller sounds of language. This fun title also presents the concepts of counting and colors. After reading, it's fun to retell the story by talking about the colors of Dog's spots and recalling how he got each one.

Driving My Tractor, by Jan Dobbins
A farmer drives his tractor and wagon across the farm, picking up animals along the way. This book is packed with options for **Have Fun With Books** and **Take Time to Rhyme**. Children love chanting the repeated phrase "Chug, chug, clank, clank, toot! It's a very busy day" while reading the book. And the accompanying CD/DVD has an illustrated version of the story that encourages children to sing along. It's also good for **Notice Print** because after the story ends, the book continues with some facts about farming, and the final page has the sheet music for the song.

I Ain't Gonna Paint No More!, by Karen Beaumont
A mischievous artist makes one big mess! The rhyming words are all body parts, the names of which most kids learn at an early age. That nearly guarantees automatic success with this story. Additionally, the whole book can be sung to the tune of the old folk song "It Ain't Gonna Rain No More," adding the element of rhythm to the already perfectly matched rhymes.

I Spy on the Farm, by Edward Gibbs
"I spy with my little eye . . . something red that begins with an R. Cock-a-doodle-doo!" Invite children to look through the hole and use the clues—color, letter, sound—to guess which animal will be revealed next. The interactive illustrations encourage young readers to play with the book by making animal noises and peeking through the cutouts. Be sure to check out the other titles in this series—they are all excellent.

Llama Llama Red Pajama, by Anna Dewdney
Comfort, fear, panic, and a satisfying resolution sum up this particular evening for a baby llama. Variations of the rhyming title repeat throughout the book along

with additional rhyming phrases. There's also excellent vocabulary, vivid and focused illustrations, and a universal story with which most kids can empathize.

Meeow and the Little Chairs, by Sebastien Braun
Meeow, a black cat, has his friends Baa, Moo, Quack, and Woof over to play. They line up different colors of chairs; Meeow rings a bell, and Moo blows his whistle. "What can they be doing? Ding-ding! Choo-choo!" They have made a train. The simple story line and bold illustrations make this a good choice for baby and toddler storytimes. Learning the concept of colors makes this a good book for **Talk Talk Talk**. Exploring the sounds like "ding" and "choo" helps young children learn and express the **Take Time to Rhyme, Sing and Play Word Games** skill. After reading, act out the story using chairs or pillows to reinforce the **Tell Stories** skill for children.

No Sleep for the Sheep!, by Karen Beaumont
Sheep is the first one to go to sleep on the farm, but she doesn't sleep for long. Soon there comes a loud "QUACK" at the door, followed by Goat's "BAA," Pig's "OINK," and so on. Once Sheep finally gets everyone to sleep in the big red barn on the farm, Rooster decides it's time to announce the dawn. Along with animal sounds, this book has great rhythm and rhymes, making it perfect for **Take Time to Rhyme, Sing and Play Word Games**.

Peck, Peck, Peck, by Lucy Cousins
Today's the day baby woodpecker learns to peck from his daddy. And once he learns, he can't seem to stop! This overzealous bird gets into the house and pecks everything he finds, including "an eggplant, a tangerine, a butter dish, a nectarine, a green bean, a sardine and seventeen jelly beans." The unusual words and rhymes make this good for young children to learn and explore the **Talk Talk Talk** and **Take Time to Rhyme** skills.

Peek-a-Moo!, by Marie Torres Cimarusti
"An oink, a moo, a cock-a-doodle-doo. Who's in the barnyard playing peek-a-boo? Guess who? 'Peek-a-moo!' says the cow." This simply illustrated lift-the-flap book plays on babies' and toddlers' fascination with peek-a-boo. Hearing and saying the rhymes and animal sounds helps children learn to recognize the smaller sounds in words, which is helpful when children begin to sound out words as they learn to read. Pointing out that the flaps are unusual helps children understand how books work, an important **Notice Print** ability.

Pete the Cat: I Love My White Shoes, by Eric Litwin
Pete is a modern classic. The catchy text invites singing along, and Pete's irrepressible attitude is engaging, encouraging readers to keep walking along and singing their songs. A variety of text features makes for an interesting discussion, especially with **Pre-Readers**. What is a thought bubble, and how is it different from regular print? What do those quotation marks tell us? And what about those musical notes on some pages?

Poem-Mobiles: Crazy Car Poems, by J. Patrick Lewis
An assortment of strange and fanciful vehicles, each given its due with a cleverly crafted poem. Read the rhymes aloud to hear the rhythms (maybe your child can guess the rhyming word!) and pore over the illustrations to talk about what you see. This book serves double duty as an example for **Notice Print All Around You** when you point out all of the words and letters in the signs, speech bubbles, and license plates.

Rain, by Carol Thompson
There are fewer things more onomatopoetic than describing a spring shower. Unusual sound combinations and simple words make this book pleasing to the ear; perfect for sharing with **Early Talkers**. You can easily combine this book with Thompson's other weather books for a whole range of experience.

Stuck in the Mud, by Jane Clarke
"'Help! Help!' clucked the hen. 'My poor little chick! He's stuck in the mud . . . and the mud's deep and thick!'" With this panicked start, Hen enlists the help of barnyard neighbors to free her wayward son. A repeated phrase, "pushed and pulled again and again," lets young readers help tell the story, and all of that pushing and pulling makes this a fun story to retell by acting it out. Great rhymes and rhythms make this a good book for **Take Time to Rhyme** as well. The use of expressive fonts (for instance, the letters in "pushed" are close together, and those in "pulled" are far apart) makes this a good one to use to explore **Notice Print**.

Where in the Wild?: Camouflaged Creatures Concealed . . . and Revealed, by David M. Schwartz and Yael Schy
There's a lot to love about this animal poetry book. It's illustrated with wonderful photos, and gatefold pages lift out to reveal where the animal is hiding. Alongside the poems, the authors have included plenty of interesting facts on each animal. A very versatile book—good for reading one poem to start off a storytime, or for sitting as a pair or in a small group and exploring for a very long time. When you're done, check out the sequel.

See the last few pages of this chapter for storytime plans for babies, toddlers, and preschoolers that use some of these books.

Connecting the Skills

For many kids, **Take Time to Rhyme** is the most difficult skill to master, yet it is one of the most important for proficient sight reading. Luckily, many of the activities **Pre-Readers** enjoy, like rhyming, singing, and wordplay, support this skill. A perfect bond between **Take Time to Rhyme** and **Have Fun With Books**! Anything caregivers can do to encourage kids to manipulate the smallest sounds in words—not syllables but individual phonemes—helps them recognize letter sounds and recall them when they occur in other words. Recommend books filled with tongue twisters or nonsensical rhymes. They are fun and help develop this skill.

Another natural pairing for **Take Time to Rhyme** is with **Talk Talk Talk**. Since we encourage caregivers to talk with their children throughout the day, why not encourage them to make up rhymes as they do? Let them make up rhymes for words they already know or words they are learning for the first time. Or even as they narrate a common task: "Put the peanut butter on the bread. I think I'll eat it in bed. So don't get it on your head!" Silly, yes, but exactly the kind of activity that will benefit a child's phonological awareness.

Links to Lifelong Learning

Take Time to Rhyme is a decoding skill. It's one of three pre-reading skills that help children garner meaning out of printed text. Once a child has mastered the 44 phonemes, there are no more to learn. However, the ability to identify and recreate those phonemes is a skill they will use time and time again throughout their life. Be it on a job application or a college entrance exam, any time a reader encounters a new word, this skill helps them decode that word for meaning. For something that begins with animal sounds and tongue twisters, **Take Time to Rhyme** is a powerhouse for a lifetime of reading.

Storytime Plans for Take Time to Rhyme, Sing and Play Word Games

The following section includes storytime plans for three age groups:

- **Early Talkers** (birth to approximately 18 months)
- **Talkers** (approximately 18 months to three years)
- **Pre-Readers** (approximately ages three to five years)

Adapt these plans to make them your own!

Take Time to Rhyme, Sing and Play Word Games: A Storytime for Early Talkers

This plan is appropriate for children birth to 18 months old with a caregiver.
   Materials you will need for this storytime:

- Music and Songs:
  - "Peek-a-Boo" (Tune: "Frère Jacques")
  - "This Is the Way We Wave Hello" (Tune: "Here We Go 'Round the Mulberry Bush")

- o "Touch Your Toes" from *Diaper Gym*, by Priscilla Hegner and Rose Grasselli
- o "My Little Hands" from *Diaper Gym*, by Priscilla Hegner and Rose Grasselli
- o "Old MacDonald Had a Farm"
- o "Brown Bear, Brown Bear, What Do You See?" from *Playing Favorites*, by Greg and Steve
- Action Rhymes:
  - o "Hickory Dickory Dock" traditional Mother Goose rhyme
  - o "This Little Cow"
  - o "Raindrops"
  - o "Criss Cross Applesauce" from *The Kingfisher Playtime Treasury*, by Pie Corbett
- Puppets (optional):
  - o Assorted farm animals appropriate for "Old MacDonald Had a Farm"
- Books:
  - o *Barnyard Banter*, by Denise Fleming
  - o *Rain, by* Carol Thompson
  - o *Brown Bear, Brown Bear, What Do You See?*, by Bill Martin Jr.

Call Everyone to Storytime

Use a rain stick or other simple instrument to gather everyone's attention, saying something like "Do you hear that? It's the sound of storytime. Time for storytime!" Once everyone is settled in place, introduce yourself and welcome everyone.

Give Opening 6 by 6 Message to Caregivers

Our books today all demonstrate the smallest sounds in words. The ability to hear these small sounds is one of the most difficult for children to learn. Hearing those sounds is important when children learn to read on their own, so they can sound words out. We can develop this skill by reading rhyming stories and singing songs. Even our first welcome song "Peek-a-Boo" has some rhyming words!

Sing the Welcome Song

"Peek-a-Boo" (Tune: "Frère Jacques")

> Peek a boo! Peek a boo!
> I see you! I see you!
> I'm so glad to see you! I'm so glad to see you!
> Peek a boo! Peek a boo!

Sing the Opening Song

"This Is the Way We Wave Hello" (Tune: "Here We Go 'Round the Mulberry Bush")

> This is the way we wave hello,
> Wave hello, wave hello.
> This is the way we wave hello
> So early in the morning!

Repeat with other actions such as clap our hands, touch our nose, tap our feet. Finish with wave hello once again.

Introduce and Read the Book

Barnyard Banter, by Denise Fleming
　　Point out title, author, and illustrator.

Introduce and Play/Sing the Song

"Old MacDonald Had a Farm"
　　Use assorted farm animal puppets to guide the song, having caregivers make the animal sounds with you. Keep puppets in a box or basket out of sight so you can control how long the song goes on; some groups will be able to sing many verses, and others will lose interest after just a couple.

Deliver 6 by 6 Message to Caregivers

It may feel silly to make animals sounds, but we do it for a reason. The letter/ sound combinations in many animal noises (in English, at least) are some of the first ones babies are able to make. Experimenting and repeating animal sounds with your child encourages her to play with sounds, letters, and the mouth movements to produce them. It also boosts her confidence when she sees a cow and can immediately say "moo."

Lead the Action Rhyme

"This Little Cow." Begin with baby in lap, facing caregiver.

> This little cow eats grass, (wiggle baby's thumb)
> This little cow eats hay. (wiggle baby's index finger)

This little cow drinks water, (wiggle baby's middle finger)
This little cow runs away. (wiggle baby's ring finger)
And this little cow does nothing at all but lie in the field all day. (wiggle baby's
    little finger)
MOO! (tickle baby)

Introduce and Play the Song

"Touch Your Toes" from *Diaper Gym*, by Priscilla Hegner and Rose Grasselli

Introduce and Play the Song

"My Little Hands" from *Diaper Gym*, by Priscilla Hegner and Rose Grasselli

Deliver 6 by 6 Message to Caregivers

We've talked about rhyming words, singing, and animal sounds. This next book
uses words that don't exactly rhyme, but the letters are similar enough in many
of them that you really have to listen to hear the differences. You can accentuate
the differences slightly as you read it aloud.

Introduce and Read the Book

Rain, by Carol Thompson

Lead the Action Rhyme

"Raindrops." Begin with baby in lap, facing caregiver.

    Pitter patter raindrops,
    Falling from the sky. (wiggle fingers down from the sky)
    Here is my umbrella (clasp fingers and hold over baby's head, elbows out)
    To keep me safe and dry! (hug baby)

Deliver 6 by 6 Message to All Participants

We are nearing the end of our storytime, so it's time for our final story and rhyme.
I hope you will check out a few books to take home and find a bit of time every
day to read together. If your baby gets fussy and doesn't want to stay calm, don't

feel bad about putting the book down and trying again later. It doesn't have to be one long stretch of time, either. Just a few minutes here and there will help them learn to love books.

Introduce the Book and Song

Brown Bear, Brown Bear, What Do You See?, by Bill Martin Jr. and "Brown Bear, Brown Bear, What Do You See?" from *Playing Favorites*, by Greg and Steve

This book is great to read aloud but can also be sung to a tune similar to "Baa Baa Black Sheep." We will listen to the song while I turn the pages.

Lead the Action Rhyme

"Criss Cross Applesauce" Begin with baby on lap, facing away from caregiver.

> Criss cross applesauce (use finger to make X on baby's back)
> Spiders crawling up your spine (crawl fingers up baby's spine)
> Cool breeze (blow on baby's neck)
> Tight squeeze (hug baby)
> Makes you get the sillies! (tickle baby)

Invite Participants to Extend Storytime

Invite them to stay and explore your library's children's area.

Take Time to Rhyme, Sing and Play Word Games: A Storytime for Talkers

This plan is appropriate for children approximately 18 months to three years old with their caregivers.

Materials you need for this storytime:

- Music and Songs:
  - Rain stick or other simple instrument
  - "The More We Get Together" (sing or find a recorded version, such as Laurie Berkner's on the album *Buzz Buzz*.)
  - "Put a Chicken on Your Head," by Eric Litwin and Michael Levine available online at The Learning Groove
  - "Storytime Is Over" (Tune: "If You're Happy and You Know It")
- Puppet or Toy:
  - Train

- Poem
  - "T-R-A-I-N" (Tune: "Bingo Was His Name-O")
- Action Rhyme:
  - "Five Little Ducks," traditional, many examples online
- Books:
  - *No Sleep for the Sheep!*, *by* Karen Beaumont
  - *Chugga-Chugga Choo-Choo*, by Kevin Lewis
  - *Pete the Cat: I Love My White Shoes*, by Eric Litwin

Call Everyone to Storytime

Use a rain stick or other simple instrument to gather everyone's attention, saying something like "Do you hear that? It's the sound of storytime. Time for storytime!" Once everyone is settled in place, introduce yourself and welcome everyone.

Give Opening 6 by 6 Message to Caregivers

Today's skill is **Take Time to Rhyme, Sing and Play Word Games**. These three activities help children learn that words are made up of smaller sounds. Knowing this and recognizing sounds is important for when children begin to learn to read, when they sound out words. Plus, it's fun!

Sing or Play the Welcome Song

"The More We Get Together," traditional.

Note: Many adults are familiar with this song. If you use Laurie Berkner's recording and are not going to post all of the lyrics, be sure to make a poster with the names that Laurie sings in her version, so adults can continue to sing along.

Introduce the Puppet/Toy

Show the train puppet or toy and say that one of today's stories features a train and we're going to do a chant about a train. Ask adults to help children clap as you recite the letters. This type of word game can help children learn to hear the smaller sounds in words.

Read/Recite the Poem

"T-R-A-I-N" (Tune: "Bingo Was His Name-O")

There is something that goes "whoo-whoo,"
And train is its name-O,
T-R-A-I-N,
T-R-A-I-N,
T-R-A-I-N,
And train is its name-O!

Repeat three or more times until most children are able to clap along in time (most likely with continued adult assistance).

Introduce the Book

No Sleep for the Sheep!, by Karen Beaumont
    Point out title, author, and illustrator.

Deliver 6 by 6 Message to Caregivers

Grown-ups, many picture books rhyme, and this one does too. It also has a wonderful rhythm, which helps children hear the smaller sounds in words.

Deliver 6 by 6 Message to All Participants

Will you help me read this book? There's a line we can say together. When I lift my finger to my lips, you do that too, and together we'll say "Shhh! Not a peep! Go to sleep!" Let's practice a few times.

Read the Book

Encourage everyone to repeat the phrase with you at the appropriate times.
    While reading, pause to briefly discuss concepts or words that may be unfamiliar to toddlers.

Transition to the Next Activity

Did you notice the duck in this book? Next, let's do a rhyme about five little ducks.

Lead the Action Rhyme

"Five Little Ducks," traditional
    Repeat once or twice.

Transition to the Next Book

Great job with our rhyme! Let's read our book about a train next.

Introduce the Book

Chugga-Chugga Choo-Choo, by Kevin Lewis
  Point out title, author, and illustrator.

Deliver 6 by 6 Message to Caregivers

Grown-ups, many children's books rhyme, and this one does, too. But it also features alliteration—which is when words start with the same sounds but end differently. Alliteration will help children learn to hear and recognize the smaller sounds that make up words.

Deliver 6 by 6 Message to All Participants

This is another book we can all read together. Can you help make the sound of a train whistle? When I lift my hand in the air, you lift yours, too and we'll say "whoooo! whoooo!" together. (You can make the motion of an engineer pulling down to sound the whistle. Lifting your fist up gives a prompt for toddlers—and adults—that it's time to whistle.)

Read the Book

Encourage everyone to participate in making the train sound when it's time.
  While reading, pause to briefly discuss concepts or words that may be unfamiliar to toddlers.

Review the Book

Did you hear all of those sounds? There were lots of "chuggas" and lots of "choos." Those two words sound the same at the beginning but different at the end. Maybe later you can think of more words that start with the "ch" sound.

Transition to the Next Activity

So that was our second book, *Chugga-Chugga Choo-Choo,* by Kevin Lewis. Next, I want to play a song that has some silly words in it: "dip dip diddly doo." Can you say that with me? "Dip dip diddly doo." Let's sing that during the song—I'll let you know when it's time. And everybody get up and do the actions with me!

Introduce and Play the Song

"Put a Chicken on Your Head," by Eric Litwin and Michael Levine
    Encourage everyone to sing and dance along.

Transition to the Next Book

Great job, everybody! Let's have a seat and get ready for our next book—it's about a cat who gets into all kinds of messes.

Introduce the Book

Pete the Cat: I Love My White Shoes, by Eric Litwin
    Point out title, author, and illustrator.

Deliver 6 by 6 Message to All Participants

This book is so much fun because you get to sing along. I'll let you know when it's time! (While reading, sing the "I love my [color] shoes" lines multiple times each, so that the children can follow along.)

Read the Book

Encourage everyone to participate in singing along.
    While reading, pause to briefly discuss concepts or words that may be unfamiliar to toddlers.

Transition to the Closing Song

So that was our third book, *Pete the Cat: I Love My White Shoes*. Can you remember all three books we read today? (Go over the titles again, in order.) Our third book was our last book for today. So we'll sing our goodbye song, and I'll see you next time!

Sing the Closing Song

"Storytime Is Over" (Tune: "If You're Happy and You Know It")

    Now storytime is over, wave goodbye.
    Now storytime is over, wave goodbye.
    Now storytime is done and I hope you had lots of fun,
    Our storytime is over, wave goodbye.

Invite Participants to Extend Storytime

Let people know they are welcome to come over to see the instrument you use for the call, or to see today's puppet. Invite them to stay and explore your library's children's area.

Take Time to Rhyme, Sing and Play Word Games: A Storytime for Pre-Readers

This plan is appropriate for children ages three to five with a caregiver. Materials you will need for this storytime:

- Music and Songs:
  - "Everybody Come and Take" (Tune: "Shortnin' Bread")
  - "If You're Happy and You Know It"
  - "If You're Wearing Red Today" (Tune: "Mary Had a Little Lamb")
  - "Storytime Is Over" (Tune: "If You're Happy and You Know It")
- Action Rhymes:
  - "Reach for the Ceiling"
  - "Jenny Paints with One Paintbrush"
  - "Hop Like a Rabbit"
- Books:
  - *Bear Sees Colors*, by Karma Wilson
  - *I Ain't Gonna Paint No More!*, by Karen Beaumont
  - *Bubble Gum, Bubble Gum*, by Lisa Wheeler

Call Everyone to Storytime

Use a rain stick or other simple instrument to gather everyone's attention, saying something like "Do you hear that? It's the sound of storytime. Time for storytime!" Once everyone is settled in place, introduce yourself and welcome everyone.

Sing the Welcome Song

"Everybody Come and Take" (Tune: "Shortnin' Bread")

> Everybody come and take
> Everybody come and take
> Everybody come and take a seat on the floor.
> Not on the ceiling,
> Not on the door,
> Everybody come and take a seat on the floor.

Sing the Opening Song

Sing a few verses of "If You're Happy and You Know It"
  Conclude with these lyrics:

> Now storytime is starting sit real still,
> Now storytime is starting sit real still,
> Your hands are in your lap, you are sitting down real flat,
> Storytime is starting sit real still.

Give Opening 6 by 6 Message to Caregivers

Today's **6 by 6** skill is **Take Time to Rhyme, Sing and Play Word Games.** Many kids who have trouble learning to read have trouble hearing the smallest sounds in words. Smaller than syllables even. I'm talking about the individual sounds of letters. Rhyming, singing, and playing with words are fun ways to practice this skill.

Introduce and Read the Book

Bear Sees Colors, by Karma Wilson

Sing or Play the Song

"If You're Wearing Red Today" (Tune: Mary Had a Little Lamb)

> If you're wearing red today, red today, red today,
> If you're wearing red today, please stand up.
> If you're wearing blue today, blue today, blue today,
> If you're wearing blue today, please stand up.
> If you're wearing green today, green today, green today,
> If you're wearing green today, please stand up.

(Continue singing colors until all children are standing.)

Lead the Action Rhyme

"Reach for the Ceiling"

> Reach for the ceiling,
> Touch the floor,
> Stand up again, let's do some more.

Touch your head,
Then your knee,
Up to your shoulders, if you please.
Clap your hands,
Stomp your feet,
Then turn around and have a seat.

Deliver 6 by 6 Message to Caregivers

There is a rhythm when we speak just like there is a rhythm in music. Reading and listening require the same focus needed to perform music. Luckily, most kids are naturally drawn to music and singing, so it is a fun, relaxed way to practice this particular early literacy skill. I'm going to sing this next book and emphasize one rhyming word and have the kids guess the next rhyming word before turning the page.

Introduce and Read the Book

I Ain't Gonna Paint No More!, by Karen Beaumont
   (Sing this book to the tune of "It Ain't Gonna Rain No More")

Lead the Action Rhyme

"Jenny Paints with One Paintbrush"

Jenny paints with one paintbrush (pretend to paint with right hand)
One paintbrush, one paintbrush.
Jenny paints with one paintbrush,
Now she paints with two. (pretend to paint with right and left hands)
Jenny paints with two paintbrushes
Two paintbrushes, two paintbrushes.
Jenny paints with two paintbrushes,
Now she paints with three. (paint with right and left hands while stomping
   right foot)
Jenny paints with three paintbrushes
Three paintbrushes, three paintbrushes.
Jenny paints with three paintbrushes,
Now she paints with four. (paint with right and left hands, stomp with right
   and left foot)
Jenny paints with four paintbrushes
Four paintbrushes, four paintbrushes.
Jenny paints with four paintbrushes,
Now she paints with five. (paint with hands, stomp with feet, nod head)
Jenny paints with five paintbrushes

Five paintbrushes, five paintbrushes.
Jenny paints with five paintbrushes,
Then she takes a break!

Lead the Action Rhyme

"Hop Like a Rabbit"

Can you hop like a rabbit?
Can you jump like a frog?
Can you walk like a duck?
Can you run like a dog?
Can you fly like a bird?
Can you swim like a fish?
Can you turn around,
Then sit like this?

Deliver 6 by 6 Message to Caregivers

We all know there are 26 letters in the English alphabet, but there are 44 distinct sounds that can be made from those letters. Those are the phonemes I mentioned earlier. You probably noticed in *I Ain't Gonna Paint No More!* that I paused before turning the page so kids could guess the next body part based on the rhyme. I'll do a similar thing with this next book but with different animals.

Introduce and Read the Book

Bubble Gum, Bubble Gum, by Lisa Wheeler

Sing the Closing Song

"Storytime Is Over" (Tune: "If You're Happy and You Know It")

Now storytime is over, wave goodbye.
Now storytime is over, wave goodbye.
Now storytime is done and I hope you had lots of fun,
our storytime is over, wave goodbye.

Invite Participants to Extend Storytime

Invite them to stay and explore your library's children's area.

TAKE TIME TO RHYME, SING AND PLAY WORD GAMES: A REPRODUCIBLE STORYTIME GUIDE FOR EARLY TALKERS

Call Everyone to Storytime

Give Opening 6 by 6 Message to Caregivers

Our books today all demonstrate the smallest sounds in words. The ability to hear these small sounds is one of the most difficult for children to learn. Hearing those sounds is important when children learn to read on their own, so they can sound words out. We can develop this skill by reading rhyming stories and singing songs. Even our first welcome song "Peek-a-Boo" has some rhyming words!

Sing the Welcome Song
"Peek-a-Boo"

Sing the Opening Song
"This Is the Way We Wave Hello"

Introduce and Read the Book
Barnyard Banter, by Denise Fleming

Introduce and Play/Sing the Song
"Old MacDonald Had a Farm"

Deliver 6 by 6 Message to Caregivers

It may feel silly to make animals sounds, but we do it for a reason. The letter/sound combinations in many animal noises (in English, at least) are some of the first ones babies are able to make. Experimenting and repeating animal sounds with your child encourages her to play with sounds, letters, and the mouth movements to produce them. It also boosts her confidence when she sees a cow and can immediately say "moo."

Lead the Action Rhyme
"This Little Cow"

Introduce and Play the Song
"Touch Your Toes" from *Diaper Gym*

Introduce and Play the Song
"My Little Hands" from *Diaper Gym*

Deliver 6 by 6 Message to Caregivers

We've talked about rhyming words, singing, and animal sounds. This next book uses words that don't exactly rhyme, but the letters are similar enough in many of them that you really have to listen to hear the differences. You can accentuate the differences slightly as you read it aloud.

Introduce and Read the Book
Rain, by Carol Thompson

Lead the Action Rhyme
"Raindrops"

Deliver 6 by 6 Message to All Participants

We are nearing the end of our storytime, so it's time for our final story and rhyme. I hope you will check out a few books to take home and find a bit of time every day to read together. If your baby gets fussy and doesn't want to stay calm, don't feel bad about putting the book down and trying again later. It doesn't have to be one long stretch of time, either. Just a few minutes here and there will help them learn to love books.

Introduce the Book and Song
Brown Bear, Brown Bear, What Do You See?, by Bill Martin Jr. and "Brown Bear, Brown Bear, What Do You See?" from *Playing Favorites*, by Greg and Steve

Lead the Action Rhyme
"Criss Cross Applesauce"

From *Six Skills by Age Six: Launching Early Literacy at the Library* by Anna Foote and Bradley Debrick. Santa Barbara, CA: Libraries Unlimited. Copyright © 2016. 129

TAKE TIME TO RHYME, SING AND PLAY WORD GAMES: A REPRODUCIBLE STORYTIME GUIDE FOR TALKERS

Call Everyone to Storytime

Give Opening 6 by 6 Message to Caregivers

Today's skill is **Take Time to Rhyme, Sing and Play Word Games**. These three activities help children learn that words are made up of smaller sounds. Knowing this and recognizing sounds is important for when children begin to learn to read, when they sound out words. Plus, it's fun!

Sing or Play the Welcome Song
"The More We Get Together," traditional.

Introduce the Puppet/Toy

Read/Recite the Poem
"T-R-A-I-N" (Tune: "Bingo Was His Name-O")

Introduce the Book
No Sleep for the Sheep!, by Karen Beaumont

Deliver 6 by 6 Message to Caregivers

Grown-ups, many picture books rhyme, and this one does too. It also has a wonderful rhythm, which helps children hear the smaller sounds in words.

Deliver 6 by 6 Message to All Participants

Will you help me read this book? There's a line we can say together. When I lift my finger to my lips, you do that too, and together we'll say "Shhh! Not a peep! Go to sleep!" Let's practice a few times.

Read the Book

Lead the Action Rhyme
"Five Little Ducks," traditional

Introduce the Book
Chugga-Chugga Choo-Choo, by Kevin Lewis

Deliver 6 by 6 Message to Caregivers

Grown-ups, many children's books rhyme, and this one does, too. But it also features alliteration—which is when words start with the same sounds but end differently. Alliteration will help children learn to hear and recognize the smaller sounds that make up words.

Deliver 6 by 6 Message to All Participants

This is another book we can all read together. Can you help make the sound of a train whistle? When I lift my hand in the air, you lift yours, too and we'll say "whoooo! whoooo!" together. (You can make the motion of an engineer pulling down to sound the whistle. Lifting your fist up gives a prompt for toddlers—and adults—that it's time to whistle.)

Read the Book

Introduce and Play the Song
"Put a Chicken on Your Head," by Eric Litwin and Michael Levine

Introduce the Book
Pete the Cat: I Love My White Shoes, by Eric Litwin

Deliver 6 by 6 Message to All Participants

This book is so much fun because you get to sing along. I'll let you know when it's time! (While reading, sing the "I love my (color) shoes" lines multiple times each, so that the children can follow along.)

Read the Book

Sing the Closing Song
"Storytime Is Over" (Tune: "If You're Happy and You Know It")

TAKE TIME TO RHYME, SING AND PLAY WORD GAMES: A REPRODUCIBLE STORYTIME GUIDE FOR PRE-READERS

Call Everyone to Storytime

Sing the Welcome Song
"Everybody Come and Take" (Tune: "Shortnin' Bread")

Sing the Opening Song
"If You're Happy and You Know It"

Give Opening 6 by 6 Message to Caregivers

Today's **6 by 6** skill is **Take Time to Rhyme, Sing and Play Word Games.** Many kids who have trouble learning to read have trouble hearing the smallest sounds in words. Smaller than syllables even. I'm talking about the individual sounds of letters. Rhyming, singing, and playing with words are fun ways to practice this skill.

Introduce and Read the Book
Bear Sees Colors, by Karma Wilson

Sing or Play the Song
"If You're Wearing Red Today" (Tune: Mary Had a Little Lamb)

Lead the Action Rhyme
"Reach for the Ceiling"

Deliver 6 by 6 Message to Caregivers

There is a rhythm when we speak just like there is a rhythm in music. Reading and listening require the same focus needed to perform music. Luckily, most kids are naturally drawn to music and singing, so it is a fun, relaxed way to practice this particular early literacy skill. I'm going to sing this next book and emphasize one rhyming word and have the kids guess the next rhyming word before turning the page.

Introduce and Read the Book
I Ain't Gonna Paint No More!, by Karen Beaumont
(Sing this book to the tune of "It Ain't Gonna Rain No More")

Lead the Action Rhyme
"Jenny Paints with One Paintbrush"

Lead the Action Rhyme
"Can You Stretch?"

Deliver 6 by 6 Message to Caregivers

We all know there are 26 letters in the English alphabet, but there are 44 distinct sounds that can be made from those letters. Those are the phonemes I mentioned earlier. You probably noticed in *I Ain't Gonna Paint No More!* that I paused before turning the page so kids could guess the next body part based on the rhyme. I'll do a similar thing with this next book but with different animals.

Introduce and Read the Book
Bubble Gum, Bubble Gum, by Lisa Wheeler

Sing the Closing Song
"Storytime Is Over" (Tune: "If You're Happy and You Know It")

Looking Ahead

Take Time to Rhyme, Sing and Play Word Games is another of the six skills children need to have experienced by about age six to be ready to learn to read. Children learn all of these skills simultaneously, beginning as soon as they are born. Rhyming, singing, and playing with words are excellent ways to help children hear the smaller sounds in words. This skill is critical for children to have as they learn to sound out words, which leads to reading fluency and comprehension.

In our next chapter, we'll discuss another of the six skills, **Notice Print All Around You**.

References

Braun, Sebastien. *Meeow and the Little Chairs*. London: Boxer Books, 2009.

Beaumont, Karen. *I Ain't Gonna Paint No More!*. Orlando, FL: Harcourt, 2005.

Beaumont, Karen. *No Sleep for the Sheep!*. Boston: Houghton Children Books, 2011.

Cimarusti, Marie Torres. *Peek-a-Moo!*. New York: Dutton's Children's Books, 1998.

Clarke, Jane. *Stuck in the Mud*. New York: Walker Pub., 2008.

Corbett, Pie. *The Kingfisher Playtime Treasury: A Collection of Playground Rhymes, Games, and Action Songs*. London: Kingfisher Books, 1989. Used with permission.

Cousins, Lucy. *Peck, Peck, Peck*. Somerville, MA: Candlewick, 2013.

Dewdney, Anna. *Llama Llama Red Pajama*. New York: Viking, 2005.

Dobbins, Jan. *Driving My Tractor*. Cambridge, MA: Barefoot Books, 2009.

Dodd, Emma. *Dog's Colorful Day: A Messy Story about Colors and Counting*. New York: Dutton Children's Books, 2001.

Fleming, Denise. *Barnyard Banter*. New York: Holt, 1994.

Gibbs, Edward. *I Spy on the Farm*. Somerville, MA: Templar Books, 2013.

Lewis, J. Patrick. *Poem-Mobiles: Crazy Car Poems*. New York: Schwartz & Wade Books, 2014.

Lewis, Kevin. *Chugga-Chugga Choo-Choo*. New York: Scholastic, 1999.

Litwin, Eric. *Pete the Cat: I Love My White Shoes*. New York: Harper, 2010.

Martin, Bill, Jr. *Brown Bear, Brown Bear, What Do You See?*. New York: H. Holt, 1992.

Thompson, Carol. *Rain*. Swindon, UK: Child's Play International, 2014.

Schwartz, David M., and Yael Schy. *Where in the Wild?: Camouflaged Creatures Concealed . . . and Revealed*. Berkeley, CA: Tricycle, 2007.

Wheeler, Lisa. *Bubble Gum, Bubble Gum*. New York: Little, Brown and Co, 2004.

Wilson, Karma. *Bear Sees Colors*. New York: Margaret K. McElderry Books, 2014.

Chapter 7

Notice Print All Around You

Notice Print All Around You is the skill called Print Awareness in the early literacy field. Children who have print awareness are able to see print in the environment, and they understand that it has meaning. **Notice Print** also means that children understand how books work and know book-related terms like "author," "illustrator," and "cover."

Notice Print is distinct from the skill explored in the next chapter, **Look for Letters Everywhere**, which means that children who are ready to learn to read can identify individual letters, their names, and the sounds they make.

Awareness: A Key to Learning This Skill

Awareness is key to helping children learn the **Notice Print** skill. When you intentionally point out print everywhere you see it, you help children become aware that print is all over our world, that it is distinct from objects and pictures, and that it has meaning. Print awareness includes recognizing not just letters, but numbers, punctuation, and symbols (such as the outline of a bicycle on green and white bike route signs).

Because **Notice Print All Around You** also includes understanding how books work, you need to help children become aware of the way we read—in our culture, from left to right and top to bottom. One way you can do this is to occasionally point to words as you read. Children also need to recognize book terms such as "author" and "illustrator," so it's important to take time to talk about those related terms when you read.

Activities That Help Children Develop This Skill

- Point to the title of the book and introduce the book: "The title of this book is . . . It was written by . . . and illustrated by . . . " Do this frequently during storytime.
- While introducing a book, hold it upside down and see if the children tell you to turn it around. If not, point out to them that you need to turn it before you read.
- Show children the fronts and backs of books, and help them understand that we read front to back, left to right, and down each page.
- Have children help turn the pages when reading.
- While reading, occasionally point to the words.
- Do action rhymes such as "Two Little Blackbirds" or "Open, Shut Them." Not only do they rhyme, but they help children develop the gross and fine motor skills needed to be able to write.
- Give children many opportunities to draw, paint, color, and scribble. This allows them to practice and advance their pre-writing skills.

- Show children words in different fonts—talk about them and how you knew to read that one word LOUDLY because the font was big or that this mark (!) made you know to end the sentence with surprise in your voice.
- Point out meaningful words in the environment. If you're talking to Billy, you might say, "Billy, this must be your jacket—I see it has your name written on the tag right here."
- Write out to-do or shopping lists with children, and let children see you reading and writing.
- Talk about any print you see in your environment—on street signs, someone's T-shirt, at the store, everywhere.

Books That Are Very Good for Notice Print All Around You

Note: Most high-quality picture books will illustrate more than one skill. These just happen to be some of our favorites to help children learn this skill.

Abigail, by Catherine Rayner
You will quickly notice that words are rarely in the same place from page to page. You have to look for them as if you were looking for Abigail's friends on the African savanna. It's important to point out some of the text as you read to help children realize the order of the words is logical and meaningful.

Actual Size, by Steve Jenkins
Jenkins uses cut-paper illustrations to show animals—or parts of animals—in their full, adult sizes. From the tiny pygmy mouse lemur to huge foot of the African elephant, children will be enchanted by seeing animals in their actual sizes. Some illustrations slip off the edges of the pages, like with the goliath frog, making for an interesting talk about how books usually work, and how this one is different. Be sure to talk about the gatefold—showing the actual size of a saltwater crocodile's mouth takes three pages! Clear and bold illustrations make this a good book for storytime, but the detailed animal facts Jenkins presents means it also works well for individual and small group reading.

Baby Faces, by Margaret Miller
Babies love looking at other babies, and this author knows it! Despite the board-book format, the baby-face photographs are large and sharp; perfect for young eyes still developing tracking abilities. The opposing pages feature pleasing pastel backgrounds with thick, black descriptive words make this a perfect title to accentuate **Notice Print**.

Backseat A-B-See, by Maria van Lieshout
Author/illustrator van Lieshout created this book as a celebration of road signs, and what a creative one it is. Each letter of the alphabet is paired with an appropriate sign, so the N page is illustrated with a circular red "NO ENTRY"

sign; O gets the familiar white on black "ONE WAY" arrow sign. In addition to being good for **Look for Letters**, this title is a great one for helping children **Notice Print**, since it uses images they see daily in the world.

Brown Bear, Brown Bear, What Do You See?, by Bill Martin Jr.
The text is consistently divided among every double-page spread making it easy to point out as you read. Many parents and caregivers will be familiar with this story, so in storytime, give them permission to say the words with you as you turn the page. Perhaps all you have to do is point to the text and they'll know what to say!

Cat Says Meow: And Other Animalopoeia, by Michael Arndt
An inventive use of white space, negative spaces, and letters to illustrate animals spelling out the sounds they make. The cow, for example, is illustrated with the letters M-O-O and some simple black shading. Spend time looking at the letters in the regular print then search for them in the stylized print of the animal shape. When using this book with **Talkers**, simply look and identify the letters; when using this book with **Pre-Readers** who may already know the alphabet, focus on how the letters are used to create the animal shape.

Click, Clack, Moo: Cows That Type, by Doreen Cronin
Farmer Brown's cows are cold at night in the barn, so they type him a note demanding electric blankets and go on a "no milk" strike until their demands are met. What will Farmer have to do to keep peace on his farm? This silly story is perfect for working on noticing print since it features the act of writing and is illustrated with various fonts. It is also rich in vocabulary words ("impossible" and "typewriter," for example) and phrases ("on strike" and "neutral party").

Driving My Tractor, by Jan Dobbins
A farmer drives his tractor and wagon across the farm, picking up animals along the way. This book is packed with opportunities to talk about **Have Fun** and for **Take Time to Rhyme**. Children love chanting the repeated phrase "Chug, chug, clank, clank, toot! It's a very busy day" while reading the book. And the accompanying CD/DVD has an illustrated version of the story that encourages children to sing along. It's also good for **Notice Print** because after the story ends, the book continues with some facts about farming, and the final page has the sheet music for the song.

Hot Rod Hamster, by Cynthia Lord
A quick study of the cover tells you this book is a remarkable example of **Notice Print All Around You.** Make note of how the title follows the arc of the wheel and how it changes color from left to right. Also note the author and illustrator names at the bottom in a different type font. Atypical use of print occurs throughout as the hamster and bulldog converse in speech bubbles and questions are posed to the reader in large italics.

Moo!, by David LaRochelle

Take one cow, one car, and one word: "moo." Follow the adventures of a cow who steals the farmer's car and goes for a wild ride. Watch as the word "moo" changes directions and size, making this a quintessential book for noticing print. How many ideas can a single word convey? Use your best expressive reading voice to find out.

Nuts to You!, by Lois Ehlert

What's worse than a mischievous squirrel circling the house, tearing up flower beds, and eating the bird feed? A mischievous squirrel who's found his way into the house! The unseen narrator relies on an inventive method to get the squirrel back outside. Be sure to point out the small names next to the various animals and plants in the illustrations. And extend the fun by exploring the "Squirrel Talk" section at the end of the book, which offers plenty of interesting facts.

One Big Building: A Counting Book about Construction, by Michael Dahl

This book uses construction machines to illustrate the concept of counting from 1 to 12. The book's design gives readers plenty of opportunity to explore counting. The 12 pages are numbered, and each page features the word written out (for example, "three"), the numeral ("3"), and the appropriate number of dots for counting. And each number page lists and illustrates a correct number of machines ("THREE dump trucks haul away the dirt."). Seeing all of the different ways to express number concepts will help children develop the **Notice Print** skill. Talking about different ways of expressing the same idea ("three") will also help children learn the **Look for Letters** skill, because knowing "same" versus "different" is an important step in developing letter recognition skills. Older children will be able to distinguish between numbers and letters.

Peek-a-Moo!, by Marie Torres Cimarusti

"An oink, a moo, a cock-a-doodle-doo. Who's in the barnyard playing peek-a-boo? Guess who? 'Peek-a-moo!' says the cow." This simply illustrated lift-the-flap book plays on babies' and toddlers' fascination with peek-a-boo. Hearing and saying the rhymes and animal sounds helps children learn to recognize the smaller sounds in words, which is helpful when children begin to sound out words as they learn to read. Pointing out that the flaps are unusual helps children understand how books work, an important **Notice Print** ability.

Pete the Cat: I Love My White Shoes, by Eric Litwin

Pete is a modern classic. The catchy text invites singing along, and Pete's irrepressible attitude is engaging, encouraging readers to keep walking along and singing their songs. A variety of text features makes for an interesting discussion, especially with **Pre-Readers**. What is a thought bubble, and how is it different from regular print? What do those quotation marks tell us? And what about those musical notes on some pages?

Put It on the List!, by Kristen Darbyshire

A family sure can run out of a lot of household materials during the week . . . cereal, shampoo, baby carrots, ice cream . . . so when anything is reported as all gone, Mom says, "Put it on the list!" What better way to get kids interested in the value of print than this book, which features list making, shopping, and familiar, everyday items!

Stuck in the Mud, by Jane Clarke

"'Help! Help!' clucked the hen. 'My poor little chick! He's stuck in the mud . . . and the mud's deep and thick!'" With this panicked start, Hen enlists the help of barnyard neighbors to free her wayward son. A repeated phrase, "pushed and pulled again and again," lets young readers help tell the story, and all of that pushing and pulling makes this a fun story to retell by acting it out. Great rhymes and rhythms make this a good book for **Take Time to Rhyme** as well. The use of expressive fonts (for instance, the letters in "pushed" are close together, and those in "pulled" are far apart) makes this a good one to use to talk about **Notice Print**.

That Is NOT a Good Idea!, by Mo Willems

A cautionary tale told partially in silent movie format and partially as a red-text warning. The main story of the hungry fox and plump goose plays out with white text on black backgrounds completely independent of the illustration. It's up to the reader to connect the words with the action. The frantic substory of the yellow goslings plays out in a more common layout, but still supports **Notice Print** by increasing the text size as emotions get more desperate.

Tip Tip Dig Dig, by Emma Garcia

Many different types of machines work together to clean up a messy vacant lot in this interactive picture book. Preschoolers of all ages will be delighted with the surprise ending, which shows the result of all that work. This is a wonderful book for beginning/middle/end because it's easy to retell the story using three two-page spreads to illustrate the process of transforming an empty lot into something much more beautiful and useful. Be sure to invite children to make the actions of the machines while you read. You might also point out the large size of the action words (lift, tip, etc.) to help children develop the **Notice Print** skill.

Tuck Me In!, by Dean Hacohen

Time for bed, baby animals! Who needs to be tucked in? One by one, Baby Pig, Baby Zebra, Baby Moose and others reply "I do!," and readers turn half-page "blankets" over the babies in their beds. Pointing out how the half pages are unusual will help children learn the ways books work, and the unusual animals featured will help build their vocabularies.

What Are You So Grumpy About?, by Tom Lichtenheld

A lot of things can go wrong in a young child's life: mom forgets to buy kid-style cereal, so he's forced to eat "grown-up" cereal; and—ew—her gravy touched her peas! "[gravy + peas = poison]." Told with humor and a happy ending, this story will have **Pre-Readers** laughing out loud. One of the treasures of this book is the varied fonts and places they are found (cereal ingredients on the sides of boxes, a chore list on the fridge), making it a great choice for featuring the **Notice Print** skill. If you like this one, be sure to check out a companion title, *Yes Day!*, that Lichtenheld created with Amy Krouse Rosenthal. *Yes Day!* celebrates the one day a year where the answer to a boy's every question is "yes!"

Where in the Wild?: Camouflaged Creatures Concealed . . . and Revealed, by David M. Schwartz and Yael Schy
There's a lot to love about this animal poetry book. It's illustrated with wonderful photos, and gatefold pages lift out to reveal where the animal is hiding. Alongside the poems, the authors have included plenty of interesting facts on each animal. A very versatile book—good for reading one poem to start off a storytime, or for sitting as a pair or in a small group and exploring for a very long time. When you're done, check out the sequel.

Where Is Baby's Belly Button?, by Karen Katz
Giant flaps, almost half the size of the page, are the perfect vehicle for young hands to manipulate and discover the print hidden underneath. An ideal experience for **Notice Print**; when the words appear, point to them and read them aloud.

See the last few pages of this chapter for storytime plans for babies, toddlers, and preschoolers that use some of these books.

Connecting the Skills

Despite **Notice Print** being one of the three decoding skills—the finite skills that are complete once mastered—it connects quite readily to several of the other **6 by 6** areas. Kids who recognize print, even when they cannot yet decode its meaning, will relish finding print in the environment and pointing it out. This ties nicely with **Have Fun With Books** because of the enjoyment they get sharing their print discoveries whether they be on a street sign or on the cover of a picture book.

You can also connect **Notice Print** with **Look for Letters** and **Take Time to Rhyme** by comparing the shape and sounds of similar looking words. Even **Talkers** who can visually distinguish letter shapes will be able to notice the same two letters on cat, mat, sat, and hat. It's then up to children to learn and use **Look for Letters** and **Take Time to Rhyme** (the other two decoding skills) to make those letters into intelligible words.

Links to Lifelong Learning

As adults, we use print awareness skills to fill out forms, read instruction manuals, and even buy the right kind of apples for a recipe. We understand so well the various shapes, sizes, colors, typesets, kerning, letter spacing, and styles that we can almost ignore the appearance and skip right to the meaning. We are masters of **Notice Print**. But we didn't become masters automatically. We got there because we understood that print had meaning even before we could read that meaning for ourselves. The more we adults talk about print conventions with new readers, the easier it will be for them to see through the details and find the importance.

Storytime Plans for Notice Print All Around You

The following section includes storytime plans for three age groups:

- **Early Talkers** (birth to approximately 18 months)
- **Talkers** (approximately ages 18 months to three years)
- **Pre-Readers** (approximately ages three to five years)

Adapt these plans to make them your own!

Notice Print All Around You: A Storytime for Early Talkers

This plan is appropriate for children birth to 18 months old with a caregiver. Materials you will need for this storytime:

- Music and Songs:
  - "Peek-a-Boo" (Tune: "Frère Jacques")
  - "This Is the Way We Wave Hello" (Tune: "Here We Go 'Round the Mulberry Bush")
  - "Touch Your Toes" from *Diaper Gym*, by Priscilla Hegner and Rose Grasselli
  - "My Little Hands" from *Diaper Gym*, by Priscilla Hegner and Rose Grasselli
  - "Brown Bear, Brown Bear, What Do You See?" from *Playing Favorites*, by Greg and Steve
- Action Rhymes:
  - "Creeping Creeping Little Flea" from *Wee Sing for Baby©*, by Pamela Conn Beall and Susan Hagen Nipp
  - "Bounce Me, Bounce Me"
  - "Cheek Chin"
- Books:
  - *Where Is Baby's Belly Button?*, by Karen Katz
  - *Baby Faces*, by Margaret Miller
  - *Brown Bear, Brown Bear, What Do You See?* By Bill Martin Jr.

Call Everyone to Storytime

Use a rain stick or other simple instrument to gather everyone's attention, saying something like "Do you hear that? It's the sound of storytime. Time for storytime!" Once everyone is settled in place, introduce yourself and welcome everyone.

Give Opening 6 by 6 Message to Caregivers

In today's storytime, we will focus on the early literacy skill **Notice Print All Around You**. For kids under two (or **Early Talkers**), it's mostly about being comfortable with books and knowing how they work. It ties in nicely with another of our early literacy skills, **Have Fun With Books**, because being aware of print and being motivated to learn to read print are so interdependent.

Sing the Welcome Song

"Peek-a-Boo" (Tune: "Frère Jacques")

> Peek a boo! Peek a boo!
> I see you! I see you!
> I'm so glad to see you!
> I'm so glad to see you! I'm so glad to see you!
> Peek a boo! Peek a boo!

Sing the Opening Song

"This Is the Way We Wave Hello" (Tune: "Here We Go 'Round the Mulberry Bush")

> This is the way we wave hello,
> Wave hello, wave hello.
> This is the way we wave hello
> So early in the morning!

Repeat with other actions such as clap our hands, touch our nose, tap our feet. Finish with wave hello once again.

Deliver 6 by 6 Message to Caregivers

Our first book today is an older book by Karen Katz called *Where Is Baby's Belly Button?* This particular board book is excellent for sharing one-on-one because part of the text is hidden under a flap on each page. When you (or your baby) pull down the flap, print magically appears that you can point to while you read it.

Introduce and Read the Book

Where Is Baby's Belly Button?, by Karen Katz
    Point out title, author, and illustrator.

Lead the Action Rhyme

"Creeping Creeping Little Flea." Begin with baby on lap, facing away from caregiver.

> Creeping, creeping little flea (creep fingers up baby's body as you name each
>   body part)
> Up my leg and past my knee
> To my tummy, on he goes
> Past my chin and to my nose.
> Now he's creeping down my chin
> To my tummy once again
> Down my leg and past my knee
> To my toe that little flea . . .
> GOTCHA! (tickle!)

Introduce and Play the Song

"Touch Your Toes" from *Diaper Gym*, by Priscilla Hegner and Rose Grasselli

Introduce and Play the Song

"My Little Hands" from *Diaper Gym*, by Priscilla Hegner and Rose Grasselli

Deliver 6 by 6 Message to Caregivers

You've probably noticed that babies love looking at other babies. This next book features up-close photographs of babies making different kinds of faces. That by itself makes this a great book to share! But why it fits so well in this storytime is because the text is on a page completely by itself, opposite the photograph.

This uncluttered layout lets you and your baby focus on one thing at a time—the print or the picture.

Introduce and Read the Book

Baby Faces, by Margaret Miller
　Point out title, author, and illustrator.

Lead the Action Rhyme

"Bounce Me, Bounce Me." Begin with baby on lap, facing caregiver.

　Bounce me, bounce me on your knee. (bounce baby gently)
　Bounce me, bounce me pretty please.
　Bounce me, bounce me here and there.
　Bounce me, bounce me in the air! (lift baby)

Lead the Action Rhyme

"Cheek Chin." Begin with baby on lap, facing caregiver.

　Cheek, chin, cheek, chin, cheek, chin, nose. (touch baby as you say
　　each word)
　Cheek, chin, cheek, chin, cheek, chin, toes.
　Cheek, chin, cheek, chin, up baby goes! (lift baby)

Deliver 6 by 6 Message to All Participants

We are nearing the end of our storytime, so it's time for our final story and rhyme. I hope you will spend some time between now and your next library visit playing with books, pointing out letters, and letting your baby see you reading.

Introduce the Book and Song

Brown Bear, Brown Bear, What Do You See?, by Bill Martin Jr. and "Brown Bear, Brown Bear, What Do You See?" from *Playing Favorites*, by Greg and Steve
　This book is great to read aloud but can also be sung to a tune similar to "Baa Baa Black Sheep." We will listen to the song while I turn the pages.

Lead the Action Rhyme

"Criss Cross Applesauce." Begin with baby on lap, facing away from caregiver.

> Criss cross applesauce (use finger to make X on baby's back)
> Spiders crawling up your spine (crawl fingers up baby's spine)
> Cool breeze (blow on baby's neck)
> Tight squeeze (hug baby)
> Makes you get the sillies! (tickle baby)

Invite Participants to Extend Storytime

Invite them to stay and explore your library's children's area.

Notice Print All Around You: A Storytime for Talkers

This plan is appropriate for children approximately 18 months to three years old with their caregivers.

Materials you will need for this storytime:

- Music and Songs:
  - Rain stick or other simple instrument
  - "The More We Get Together" (sing or find a recorded version, such as Laurie Berkner's on the album *Buzz Buzz*.)
  - "One, Two, Buckle My Shoe," by Hap Palmer from the album *Early Childhood Classics*
  - "Storytime Is Over" (Tune: "If You're Happy and You Know It")
- Poem with Flannel/Magnet Board Set:
  - "This Little Chick"—author unknown, available online. (It's the one that starts with "This little chick is black")
- Action Rhyme:
  - "Two Little Blackbirds," traditional
- Books:
  - *Stuck in the Mud*, by Jane Clarke
  - *Driving My Tractor*, by Jan Dobbins
  - *Peek-a-Moo!*, by Marie Torres Cimarusti

Call Everyone to Storytime

Use a rain stick or other simple instrument to gather everyone's attention, saying something like "Do you hear that? It's the sound of storytime. Time for storytime!" Once everyone is settled in place, introduce yourself and welcome everyone.

Give Opening 6 by 6 Message to Caregivers

Today's skill is **Notice Print All Around You**. Noticing print means children see print all around them and understand that it has meaning. It also means that children know how to handle books—that in English, books open from the right to the left, and we read from left to right and top to bottom.

Sing or Play the Welcome Song

"The More We Get Together," traditional.

Note: Many adults are familiar with this song. If you use Laurie Berkner's recording and are not going to post all of the lyrics, be sure to make a poster with the names that Laurie sings in her version, so adults can continue to sing along.

Introduce and Recite the Flannelboard Poem

"This Little Chick," available online.

Say that today's poem is about a few colored chicks who live by a big red barn, because today we have three stories about farms and farm animals.

As you recite the poem, put the appropriate pieces up on the flannel or magnet board. Repeat once or twice.

Introduce the Book

Stuck in the Mud, by Jane Clarke

Point out title, author, and illustrator.

Deliver 6 by 6 Message to Caregivers

Grown-ups, researchers have found that up to 95 percent of children's attention is focused on the pictures, so occasionally pointing out words helps children understand that you're reading the words and not just the pictures. So when I read this book, I'll point to some of the words as I read.

Deliver 6 by 6 Message to All Participants

Everyone, here's a book you can help me read. When I say "pushed and pulled again and again," do the motions with me. (Practice lifting hands and making pushing and pulling motions.)

Read the Book

While reading, occasionally underline the words with your finger as you read them.

While reading, pause to briefly discuss concepts or words that may be unfamiliar to toddlers.

Transition to the Next Activity

So that was our first book, *Stuck in the Mud*, by Jane Clarke. Hearing the story about that hen reminds me of a good song I know about a hen. Let's listen to it! Please dance with me, and we can all count to ten when the song says.

Introduce and Play the Song

"One, Two, Buckle My Shoe," by Hap Palmer
    Encourage everyone to dance and count together.

Transition to the Next Book

Great job, everybody! Let's all sit and get ready to read our second book.

Introduce the Book

Driving My Tractor, by Jan Dobbins

Deliver 6 by 6 Message to All Participants

This is another great book for all of us to read together. There's a part where we'll say, "Chug, chug, clank, clank, toot!" Can you say that with me? (Practice a few times.) Great! I'll let you know when to say it during the story.

Read or Play the Book

If you choose to play the audio of the book, hold up the book for all to see, turning the pages when appropriate and occasionally underlining words with your finger. Encourage everyone to participate in saying the repeated phrase with you.

Review the Book

Show the group the two-page spread that ends with "It's a very busy day. PHEW!" and say, "So that's the end of the story, but look, it's not the end of the book. There are a few more pages that give facts about farms. Most books end when the story does, but this one is special. We don't have time to read the extra pages now, but if you want to look at them, come see me when storytime is finished."

Transition to the Next Activity

So that was our second book, *Driving My Tractor* by Jan Dobbins. Did you see the blackbirds in the book? (Show one of the pages with blackbirds, and point them out.) Seeing those blackbirds reminds me of a rhyme we can do together. Let's do it now!

Lead the Group in the Action Rhyme

"Two Little Blackbirds," traditional, with additional verses by Anna Foote

> Two little blackbirds sitting on a hill
> One named Jack; the other named Jill
> Fly away, Jack! Fly away, Jill!
> Come back, Jack! Come back, Jill!
> Continue with two to three of the verses below.
> Two little cows sitting on a hill
> One named Moo; the other named Boo
> Run away, Moo! Run away, Boo!
> Come back Moo! Come back Boo!
> Two little pigs sitting on a hill
> One named Oink; the other named Zoink
> Run away, Oink! Run away, Zoink!
> Come back, Oink! Come back, Zoink!
> Two little sheep sitting on a hill
> One named Baa; the other named Laa
> Run away, Baa! Run away, Laa!
> Come back, Baa! Come back, Laa!
> Two little chickens sitting on a hill
> One named Cluck; the other named Pluck
> Run away, Cluck! Run away, Pluck!
> Come back, Cluck! Come back, Pluck!
> Repeat selected verses two to three times.

Transition to the Next Book

Great, everybody! We have one more farm book, and this one is special because I will move some flaps to make the book work.

Introduce the Book

Peek-a-Moo! by Marie Torres Cimarusti

Start by holding the book upside down, and see if anyone corrects you. You might prompt the children by saying something like "So now we're ready to read . . . are we ready to read? What's wrong? . . . Oh, so I need to turn the book over to read it. That's right, like this, and the cover opens this way . . ."

Read the Book

Encourage everyone to participate in making the animal sounds as you read.

While reading, pause to briefly discuss concepts or words that may be unfamiliar to toddlers.

Transition to the Closing Song

So that was our third book, *Peek-a-Moo!*, by Marie Torres Cimarusti. Can you remember all three books we read today?" Go over the titles again, in order. "Our third book was our last book for today. So we'll sing our goodbye song, and I'll see you next time!

Sing the Closing Song

"Storytime Is Over" (Tune: "If You're Happy and You Know It")

> Now storytime is over, wave goodbye.
> Now storytime is over, wave goodbye.
> Now storytime is done and I hope you had lots of fun,
> Our storytime is over, wave goodbye.

Invite Participants to Extend Storytime

Let people know they are welcome to come over to see the instrument you use for the call, or to see today's puppet. Invite them to stay and explore your library's children's area.

Notice Print All Around You: A Storytime for Pre-Readers

This plan is appropriate for children ages three to five with a caregiver. Materials you will need for this storytime:

- Music and Songs:
  - "Everybody Come and Take" (Tune: "Shortnin' Bread")
  - "If You're Happy and You Know It"
  - "Twinkle Twinkle Little Star"
  - "Shake Your Sillies Out," by Raffi
  - "Storytime Is Over" (Tune: "If You're Happy and You Know It")
- Action Rhymes:
  - "Hurry Hurry Drive the Racecar"
  - "Wiggle Your Fingers"
  - "Hop Like a Rabbit"
- Books:
  - *Hot Rod Hamster*, by Cynthia Lord
  - *Abigail*, by Catherine Rayner
  - *That Is NOT a Good Idea!*, by Mo Willems

Call Everyone to Storytime

Use a rain stick or other simple instrument to gather everyone's attention, saying something like "Do you hear that? It's the sound of storytime. Time for storytime!" Once everyone is settled in place, introduce yourself and welcome everyone.

Sing the Welcome Song

"Everybody Come and Take" (Tune: "Shortnin' Bread")

> Everybody come and take
> Everybody come and take
> Everybody come and take a seat on the floor.
> Not on the ceiling,
> Not on the door,
> Everybody come and take a seat on the floor.

Sing the Opening Song

Sing a few verses of "If You're Happy and You Know It"
  Conclude with these lyrics:

> Now storytime is starting sit real still,
> Now storytime is starting sit real still,

Your hands are in your lap, you are sitting down real flat,
Storytime is starting sit real still.

Give Opening 6 by 6 Message to Caregivers

Notice Print All Around You is more than simply looking for print in the environment. The skill also includes knowing how books work, understanding that print has meaning, and realizing that print can be read even if it looks different.

Introduce and Read the Book

Hot Rod Hamster, by Cynthia Lord

Here's our first book, *Hot Rod Hamster*. Let's just look at the cover. What do you think the book will be about? Why do you think that? Do you notice any words on the cover? The title curves around the top of the cover and the author and illustrator names curve around the bottom. Let's read it and find out what happens.

Discuss the Book

A lot of things happen with the print in that book. It changes size and style a lot, sometimes it's in different colors, and sometimes it's in speech bubbles. The speech bubbles reinforce **Notice Print** because they directly connect the words you are reading to the character who says them. This introduces the concept of dialogue.

Lead the Action Rhyme

"Hurry Hurry Drive the Racecar" (Tune: "Ten Little Indians")

Hurry hurry drive the racecar. (pretend to turn steering wheel)
Hurry hurry drive the racecar.
Hurry hurry drive the racecar.
We will win first place!
Push the pedal, let's go faster. (use right foot to press pretend accelerator
    while steering)
Push the pedal, let's go faster.
Push the pedal, let's go faster.
We will win first place!

Look behind you, pass the others. (turn head to look over shoulder while
    steering)
Look behind you, pass the others.
Look behind you, pass the others.
We will win first place!
Hurry hurry drive the racecar. (steer the wheel much faster!)
Hurry hurry drive the racecar.
Hurry hurry drive the racecar.
We have won first place! (applause)

Lead the Action Rhyme

"Wiggle Your Fingers" (suit actions to words)

Wiggle your fingers.
Wiggle your toes.
Wiggle your ears.
Wiggle your nose.
Now all the wiggles are out of me
and I'm as quiet as I can be.

Introduce and Read the Book

Abigail, by Catherine Rayner

Play or Sing the Song

"Twinkle Twinkle Little Star"

Deliver 6 by 6 Message to Caregivers

You've probably noticed that once in a while I'll point out words as I read them.
I especially like to do that when the print isn't in a typical line going from left to
right. I want to make sure everyone understands that I'm reading the words that
look different in the same way I'm reading the "normal" words we are used to seeing.

Play or Sing the Song

"Shake Your Sillies Out," by Raffi

Lead the Action Rhyme

"Hop Like a Rabbit"

> Can you hop like a rabbit?
> Can you jump like a frog?
> Can you walk like a duck?
> Can you run like a dog?
> Can you fly like a bird?
> Can you swim like a fish?
> Can you turn around,
> Then sit like this?

Deliver 6 by 6 Message to Caregivers

Our last book today works great for **Notice Print** because the print and the picture are on opposite pages for about half the book. It really gives you a chance to notice the words, read them aloud, and then connect their meaning to the picture on the other side. There are also examples of the words changing style and color.

Introduce and Read the Book

That Is NOT a Good Idea!, by Mo Willems

Sing the Closing Song

"Storytime Is Over" (Tune: "If You're Happy and You Know It")

> Now storytime is over, wave goodbye.
> Now storytime is over, wave goodbye.
> Now storytime is done and I hope you had lots of fun,
> Our storytime is over, wave goodbye.

Invite Participants to Extend Storytime

Invite them to stay and explore your library's children's area.

NOTICE PRINT ALL AROUND YOU: A REPRODUCIBLE STORYTIME GUIDE FOR EARLY TALKERS

Call Everyone to Storytime

Give Opening 6 by 6 Message to Caregivers

In today's storytime, we will focus on the early literacy skill **Notice Print All Around You**. For kids under two (or **Early Talkers**), it's mostly about being comfortable with books and knowing how they work. It ties in nicely with another of our early literacy skills, **Have Fun With Books**, because being aware of print and being motivated by print are so interdependent.

Sing the Welcome Song
"Peek-a-Boo"

Sing the Opening Song
"This Is the Way We Wave Hello"

Deliver 6 by 6 Message to Caregivers

Our first book today is an older book by Karen Katz called *Where Is Baby's Belly Button?* This particular board book is excellent for sharing one-on-one because part of the text is hidden under a flap on each page. When you (or your baby) pull down the flap, print magically appears that you can point to while you read it.

Introduce the Book
Where Is Baby's Belly Button?, by Karen Katz

Lead the Action Rhyme
"Creeping Creeping Little Flea"

Introduce and Play the Song
"Touch Your Toes" from *Diaper Gym*

Introduce and Play the Song
"My Little Hands" from *Diaper Gym*

Deliver 6 by 6 Message to Caregivers

You've probably noticed that babies love looking at other babies. This next book features up-close photographs of babies making different kinds of faces. That by itself makes this a great book to share! But why it fits so well in this storytime is because the text is on a page completely by itself, opposite the photograph.

From *Six Skills by Age Six: Launching Early Literacy at the Library* by Anna Foote and Bradley Debrick. Santa Barbara, CA: Libraries Unlimited. Copyright © 2016. 155

This uncluttered layout lets you and your baby focus on one thing at a time—the print or the picture.

Introduce the Book
Baby Faces, by Margaret Miller

Lead the Action Rhyme
"Bounce Me, Bounce Me"

Lead the Action Rhyme
"Cheek Chin"

Deliver 6 by 6 Message to All Participants

We are nearing the end of our storytime, so it's time for our final story and rhyme. I hope you will spend some time between now and your next library visit playing with books, pointing out letters, and letting your baby see you reading.

Introduce the Book and Song
Brown Bear, Brown Bear, What Do You See?, by Bill Martin Jr. and "Brown Bear, Brown Bear, What Do You See?" from *Playing Favorites*, by Greg and Steve

Lead the Action Rhyme
"Criss Cross Applesauce"

NOTICE PRINT ALL AROUND YOU: A REPRODUCIBLE STORYTIME GUIDE FOR TALKERS

Call Everyone to Storytime

Give Opening 6 by 6 Message to Caregivers

Today's skill is **Notice Print All Around You**. Noticing print means children see print all around them and understand that it has meaning. It also means that children know how to handle books—that in English, books open from the right to the left, and we read from left to right and top to bottom.

Sing or Play the Welcome Song
"The More We Get Together," traditional.

Introduce and Recite the Flannelboard Poem
"This Little Chick," available online.

Introduce the Book
Stuck in the Mud by Jane Clarke

Deliver 6 by 6 Message to Caregivers

Grown-ups, researchers have found that up to 95 percent of children's attention is focused on the pictures, so occasionally pointing out words helps children understand that you're reading the words and not just the pictures. So when I read this book, I'll point to some of the words as I read.

Deliver 6 by 6 Message to All Participants

Everyone, here's a book you can help me read. When I say "pushed and pulled again and again," do the motions with me. (Practice lifting hands and making pushing and pulling motions.)

Read the Book

Introduce and Play the Song
"One, Two, Buckle My Shoe," by Hap Palmer

Introduce the Book
Driving My Tractor, by Jan Dobbins

Deliver 6 by 6 Message to All Participants

This is another great book for all of us to read together. There's a part where we'll say, "Chug, chug, clank, clank, toot!" Can you say that with me? (Practice a few times.) Great! I'll let you know when to say it during the story.

Read or Play the Book

If you choose to play the audio of the book, hold up the book for all to see, turning the pages when appropriate and occasionally underlining words with your finger. Encourage everyone to participate in saying the repeated phrase with you.

Lead the Group in the Action Rhyme
"Two Little Blackbirds," traditional, with additional verses by Anna Foote

Introduce and Read the Book
Peek-a-Moo!, by Marie Torres Cimarusti

Sing the Closing Song
"Storytime Is Over" (Tune: "If You're Happy and You Know It")

From *Six Skills by Age Six: Launching Early Literacy at the Library* by Anna Foote and Bradley Debrick.

158   Santa Barbara, CA: Libraries Unlimited. Copyright © 2016.

NOTICE PRINT ALL AROUND YOU: A REPRODUCIBLE STORYTIME GUIDE FOR PRE-READERS

Call Everyone to Storytime

Sing the Welcome Song
"Everybody Come and Take" (Tune: "Shortnin' Bread")

Sing the Opening Song
"If You're Happy and You Know It"

Give Opening 6 by 6 Message to Caregivers

Notice Print All Around You is more than simply looking for print in the environment. The skill also includes knowing how books work, understanding that print has meaning, and realizing that print can be read even if it looks different.

Introduce and Read the Book

Hot Rod Hamster, by Cynthia Lord
Here's our first book, *Hot Rod Hamster.* Let's just look at the cover. What do you think the book will be about? Why do you think that? Do you notice any words on the cover? The title curves around the top of the cover and the author and illustrator names curve around the bottom. Let's read it and find out what happens.

Discuss the Book

A lot of things happen with the print in that book. It changes size and style a lot, sometimes it's in different colors, and sometimes it's in speech bubbles. The speech bubbles reinforce **Notice Print** because they directly connect the words you are reading to the character who says them. That introduces the concept of dialogue.

Lead the Action Rhyme
"Hurry Hurry Drive the Racecar" (Tune: "Ten Little Indians")

Lead the Action Rhyme
"Wiggle Your Fingers"

Introduce and Read the Book
Abigail, by Catherine Rayner

Play or Sing the Song
"Twinkle Twinkle Little Star"

From *Six Skills by Age Six: Launching Early Literacy at the Library* by Anna Foote and Bradley Debrick.
Santa Barbara, CA: Libraries Unlimited. Copyright © 2016.   159

Deliver 6 by 6 Message to Caregivers

You've probably noticed that once in a while I'll point out words as I read them. I especially like to do that when the print isn't in a typical line going from left to right. I want to make sure everyone understands that I'm reading the words that look different in the same way I'm reading the "normal" words we are used to seeing.

Play or Sing the Song
"Shake Your Sillies Out," by Raffi

Lead the Action Rhyme
"Can You Stretch?"

Deliver 6 by 6 Message to Caregivers

Our last book today works great for **Notice Print** because the print and the picture are on opposite pages for about half the book. It really gives you a chance to notice the words, read them aloud, and then connect their meaning to the picture on the other side. There are also examples of the words changing style and color.

Introduce and Read the Book
That Is NOT a Good Idea! by Mo Willems

Sing the Closing Song
"Storytime Is Over" (Tune: "If You're Happy and You Know It")

Looking Ahead

Notice Print All Around You is another of the early literacy skills children need to have experienced by about age six to be ready to learn to read. Children learn all of these skills at once, beginning at birth, as we read, sing, and play with them. **Notice Print All Around You** means that children are able to recognize print wherever they see it and that they understand how books and reading work. Learning this skill helps children understand the fundamentals of reading and its significance.

In our next chapter, we'll discuss another of the six skills, **Look for Letters Everywhere**.

References

Arndt, Michael. *Cat Says Meow: And Other Animalopoeia*. San Francisco: Chronicle, 2014.

Beall, Pamela Conn and Susan Hagen Nipp. *Wee Sing for Baby*. New York: Price Stern Sloan, an imprint of Penguin Young Readers Group, 2002. Used with permission.

Cimarusti, Marie Torres. *Peek-a-Moo!*. New York: Dutton's Children's Books, 1998.

Clarke, Jane. *Stuck in the Mud*. New York: Walker Pub., 2008.

Cronin, Doreen. *Click, Clack, Moo: Cows That Type*. New York: Simon & Schuster Books for Young Readers, 2000.

Dahl, Michael. *One Big Building: A Counting Book about Construction*. Minneapolis, MN: Picture Window Books, 2004.

Darbyshire, Kristen. *Put It on the List!*. New York: Dutton Children's Books, 2009.

Dobbins, Jan. *Driving My Tractor*. Cambridge, MA: Barefoot Books, 2009.

Ehlert, Lois. *Nuts to You!*. San Diego: Harcourt Brace Jovanovich, 1993.

Garcia, Emma. *Tip Tip Dig Dig*. London: Boxer, 2007.

Hacohen, Dean, and Sherry Scharschmidt. *Tuck Me In!*. Somerville, MA: Candlewick Press, 2010.

Jenkins, Steve. *Actual Size*. Boston: Houghton Mifflin, 2004.

Katz, Karen. *Where Is Baby's Belly Button?*. New York: Little Simon, 2000.

LaRochelle, David. *Moo!*. New York: Walker Books for Young Readers, 2013.

Lichtenheld, Tom. *What Are You So Grumpy About?*. Boston: Little, Brown, 2003.

Litwin, Eric. *Pete the Cat: I Love My White Shoes*. New York: Harper, 2010.

Lord, Cynthia. *Hot Rod Hamster*. New York: Scholastic Press, 2010.

Martin, Bill. *Brown Bear, Brown Bear, What Do You See?*. New York: H. Holt, 1992.

Miller, Margaret. *Baby Faces*. New York: Little Simon, 1998.

Rayner, Catherine. *Abigail*. Wilton, CT: Tiger Tales, 2013.

Rosenthal, Amy Krouse, and Tom Lichtenheld. *Yes Day!*. New York: HarperCollins, 2009.

Schwartz, David M., and Yael Schy. *Where in the Wild?: Camouflaged Creatures Concealed . . . and Revealed*. Berkeley, CA: Tricycle Press, 2007.

Van Lieshout, Maria. *Backseat A-B-See*. San Francisco: Chronicle Books, 2012.

Willems, Mo. *That Is NOT a Good Idea!*. New York: Balzer & Bray, 2013.

Chapter 8

Look for Letters Everywhere

©2009 by the Johnson County Library

Look for Letters Everywhere is known as Letter Knowledge in the early literacy field. Basically, it means that children who are ready to learn to read can identify individual letters, their names, and the sounds they make.

Observation: A Key to Learning This Skill

Observation skills are important for children who are learning to **Look for Letters**. To be able to recognize letters, children need to be able to observe and recognize the similarities and differences among them. So one of the best pre-reading skills we can teach children is to look at objects (and eventually letters) and compare and contrast how they look.

Learning letter names and sounds involves this process: Babies learn "same" versus "different"; toddlers learn the names of shapes (the building blocks of letters); preschoolers learn the names of letters and eventually their sounds.

To be able to name the letters, children first need to be able to distinguish shapes (such as circle, square, rectangle), which are the building blocks of letters. To be able to identify shapes, children need to recognize how two or more items are the same and how they differ.

Once children have progressed through these stages and are able to name letters, they are ready to learn to identify the sound that each letter makes. They are then well on their way to sounding out words and reading!

This child is too young to know the alphabet, but he is the perfect age to play with shapes and learn how they are the same or different.

Activities That Help Children Develop This Skill

- Ask age-appropriate questions that lead into learning letter shapes and sounds. Learning letter names and sounds involves this process: Babies learn "same" versus "different"; toddlers learn the names of shapes (the building blocks of letters); preschoolers learn the names of letters and eventually their sounds.
- Frequently ask children if two objects are the same or different, then talk about ways they might be the same and ways they might be different.
- Point out shapes you see in books and around you—what shape is that slice of pizza? That ball?
- Give children puzzles of shapes and letters to solve.
- Make paper cutouts of several copies of various shapes, and work with children to sort them by shape.
- Help children make shapes and letters out of clay, in shaving cream, in fingerpaint.
- Use words that all begin with the same sound, like "Baby bounced bravely by." Talk about the letter sound, and write it down.
- Name a letter of the day—listen for words that begin with that sound, and point out when you hear that sound. Start with the sounds of letters, not their names or images. Children can recognize sounds before they can associate them with written letters.
- Cut textured letters to use for rubbings. Sandpaper and crumpled aluminum foil both work well. Put paper on top of the letters and rub over them chalk or crayon.
- Talk about the letters you see, what they are called, and the sounds they make.

Books That Are Very Good for Look for Letters Everywhere

Note: Most high-quality picture books will illustrate more than one skill. These just happen to be some of our favorites to help children learn this skill.

Alphablock, by Christopher Franceschelli
This chunky board book has few words, but children of all ages will enjoy its clever design. Large die-cut letters provide a great chance to **Look for Letters**, and the letters give a clue as to what the next word will be. For example, N sits on a tree branch, next to a bird with a twig in its mouth. "N is for . . . " (turn the page) "NEST." The short, single-word answers paired with clear illustrations will have **Pre-Readers** recognizing words by sight.

Away We Go!, by Chiêu Anh Urban
A remarkable vehicle (no pun intended!) to talk about shapes and how they are used in the illustration. The cover itself employs circles, diamonds, triangles, hearts, semicircles, and squares to create a boldly colored rocket. The shapes

support **Look for Letters** while all the vehicles and subject-specific words you can **Talk Talk Talk** about will develop a rich vocabulary.

Backseat A-B-See, by Maria van Lieshout
Author/illustrator van Lieshout created this book as a celebration of road signs, and what a creative one it is. Each letter of the alphabet is paired with an appropriate sign, so the N page is illustrated with a circular red "NO ENTRY" sign; O gets the familiar white on black "ONE WAY" arrow sign. In addition to being good for **Look for Letters**, this title is a great one for helping children **Notice Print**, since it uses images they see daily in the world.

Chicka Chicka Boom Boom, by Bill Martin Jr. and John Archambault
It's easy to look for letters in this beloved book—they're the main characters after all! The rhyming text is primed for chanting, and after a single reading, children will be chanting along as adults read. This book reminds readers to talk about letters because it features a mixture of uppercase and lowercase letters, along with letters in nontraditional positions (sideways, upside down, "knotted like a tie").

Digger, Dozer, Dumper, by Hope Vestergaard
"Trucks that sweep and dig and shift./Trucks that dump and tow and lift." From street sweeper to excavator to cherry picker, this book offers engaging rhyming poems about 16 different machines. This one is great for building vocabulary—in addition to listing the names of various machines, there are plenty of complementary words like "asphalt," "rig," and "cargo." Good for reading a poem at a time, though some readers will want to devour the book in one sitting. Extend the fun by exploring the book's final question, "Which truck would YOU like to be?"

Dino Shapes, by Suse MacDonald
The thick, sturdy pages of this board book allow even the youngest reader to feel the die-cut shapes that eventually reveal a dinosaur. Touching, turning, and experiencing shapes from a very early age supports alphabet knowledge, also known as **Look for Letters.**

Dinosaur Roar!, by Paul Stickland and Henrietta Stickland
Rhyming couplets present all kinds of dinosaurs and their behaviors: "Dinosaur roar, dinosaur squeak/dinosaur fierce, dinosaur meek . . ." Help children learn the **Look for Letters** skill by exploring the idea of opposites presented in the book, and help them learn vocabulary by talking about some of the unusual words—just what does "meek" mean, anyway? The high-interest subject and bright, large illustrations make this a good group storytime book.

Duck! Rabbit!, by Amy Krouse Rosenthal and Tom Lichtenheld
Is it a duck? Or a rabbit? Two unseen narrators argue over whether the story's strange character is a duck or a rabbit. One is sure the odd animal is acting like a duck; the other is positive it's behaving like a rabbit. This book invites interaction and debate, leaving readers with plenty to compare, contrast, and discuss.

Eating the Alphabet, by Lois Ehlert
A wonderful alphabet book from a master of collage illustration, replete with fruits and vegetables. Many alphabet books don't have a storyline, making them great for busy toddlers because they invite readers to look at a page for a minute or two and then move on. Try starting with the first letter of a child's name, or in storytime maybe the L page, since L is for library.

Go Away, Big Green Monster!, by Ed Emberley
This classic book uses die-cut pages to make a monster's face appear and then disappear, feature by feature. Children feel empowered to tell the monster to "Go away!" one feature at time. Exploring the names of facial features builds vocabulary for young children and the die-cuts make for fun discussion of the shapes you can see in this book. This is a wonderful story for retelling by using a puppet, felt board, or pieces of paper. Be sure to check out Emberley's companion title, *Nighty Night, Little Green Monster*.

Go, Shapes, Go!, by Denise Fleming
Using a hodgepodge of shapes that repeat on each page, part by part a familiar animal is formed. **Early Talkers** and **Talkers** will enjoy following the tiny mouse as it zooms around the pages, and eventually they will start to notice the shapes and how they are used. (**Pre-Readers** will recognize the animal right away and be pleased that they are "in" on the surprise before it happens!) Also of note is the simple ABCB rhyme pattern that the author splits across the page break.

Huff & Puff: Can You Blow Down the Houses of the Three Little Pigs?, by Claudia Rueda
Many children are familiar with the story of the Three Little Pigs, but this simple book invites readers into the story to play the role of the Big Bad Wolf. Die-cuts in the pages show readers just where to huff and puff and blow houses down. But fortunately Wolf is unable to blow down the final house, for there is a surprise waiting inside. The various construction materials give readers plenty to discuss. For example, why does the brick house stand when the others fall?

I Spy on the Farm, by Edward Gibbs
"I spy with my little eye . . . something red that begins with an R. Cock-a-doodle-doo!" Invite children to look through the hole and use the clues—color, letter, sound—to guess which animal will be revealed next. The interactive illustrations encourage young readers to play with the book by making animal noises and peeking through the cutouts. Be sure to check out the other titles in this series—they are all excellent.

LMNO Peas, by Keith Baker
This imaginative alphabet book features peas as the main characters, and lists and shows lots of their occupations. Take the B page for example, "B: We're builders, bathers, and bikers in a race." Readers will get a kick out of exploring the funny illustrations of peas driving cars, playing a saxophone, and parachuting from the sky (to name a few). Great for **Look for Letters** and **Talk Talk Talk**.

One Big Building: A Counting Book about Construction, by Michael Dahl
This book uses construction machines to illustrate the concept of counting from 1 to 12. The book's design gives readers plenty of opportunity to explore counting. The 12 pages are numbered, and each page features the word written out (for example, "three"), the numeral ("3"), and the appropriate number of dots for counting. And each number page lists and illustrates a correct number of machines ("THREE dump trucks haul away the dirt."). Seeing all of the different ways to express number concepts will help children develop the **Notice Print** skill. Talking about different ways of expressing the same idea ("three") will also help children learn the **Look for Letters** skill, because knowing "same" versus "different" is an important step in developing letter recognition skills. Older children will be able to distinguish between numbers and letters.

Perfect Square, by Michael Hall
As a week goes by, a perfectly happy square is transformed into a variety of shapes and objects. A sad-happy-sad-happy book that introduces several shapes (circles, triangles, rectangles, and trapezoids) created from this one perfect square. Look at how they are used, and look where they end up from one page to the next. Basic geometric shapes are the building blocks of alphabet letters.

The Sleepy Little Alphabet: A Bedtime Story from Alphabet Town, by Judy Sierra
As in *Chicka Chicka Boom Boom*, the letters are characters in this rhyming bedtime story. And just like the kids at the end of *Chicka Chicka*, these little ones aren't ready for bed: "Uh-oh! A is wide awake. And B still has a bath to take." The humor and rhythm of this book make it a good storytime choice and an excellent companion to Martin and Archambault's book.

Tip Tip Dig Dig, by Emma Garcia
Many different types of machines work together to clean up a messy vacant lot in this interactive picture book. Preschoolers of all ages will be delighted with the surprise ending, which shows the result of all that work. This is a wonderful book for beginning/middle/end because it's easy to retell the story using three two-page spreads to illustrate the process of transforming an empty lot into something much more beautiful and useful. Be sure to invite children to make the actions of the machines while you read. You might also point out the large size of the action words (lift, tip, etc.) to help children develop the ability to **Notice Print**.

See the last few pages of this chapter for storytime plans for babies, toddlers, and preschoolers that use some of these books.

Connecting the Skills

For many people, alphabet knowledge is synonymous with literacy. Of course, those of us in the profession know there is much more involved in learning to read than just reciting the 26 letters in a sing-song style. However, **Look for Letters** is a basic tenet of early literacy that connects rather logically with several of the other pre-reading skills. In fact, **Take Time to Rhyme** is not even possible without a foundation of letter knowledge. Learning the alphabet typically occurs in three steps: (1) names of letters, (2) shapes of letters, and (3) sounds of letters. Notice the natural connection between **Look for Letters** and **Take Time to Rhyme**?

Another somewhat obvious connection is with **Notice Print** because where there is print, there are letters. Finding those letters in signs and on vehicles becomes a game that supports letter knowledge and the idea that the words created by those letters are important.

You can also draw parallels between **Look for Letters** and **Tell Stories**. The alphabet is, after all, a sequence with a specific beginning, middle, and end. Publishers have recently released some excellent books that have a strong narrative woven around the alphabet concept.

Links to Lifelong Learning

As a decoding skill—one that deciphers symbols into meaning—**Look for Letters** is a finite skill that can be mastered. As you can see from the connections listed above, **Look for Letters** is a foundational skill that supports most of the others, so its direct links to lifelong learning are murky. You can likely think of dozens of applications where alphabetizing skills are needed throughout childhood and on into adulthood. (For library workers, entire parts of the world are built around the alphabet!) Some preliminary studies have even suggested that thorough knowledge of the English alphabet aids in learning a foreign language. Whether or not the recall of alphabet letters is specifically required in day-to-day adulthood, it is safe to say **Look for Letters** is an essential skill for literacy.

Storytime Plans for Look for Letters Everywhere

The following section includes storytime plans for three age groups:

- **Early Talkers** (birth to approximately 18 months)
- **Talkers** (approximately 18 months to three years)
- **Pre-Readers** (approximately ages three to five years)

Adapt these plans to make them your own!

Look for Letters Everywhere: A Storytime for Early Talkers

This plan is appropriate for children birth to 18 months old with a caregiver. Materials you will need for this storytime:

- Music and Songs:
  - "Peek-a-Boo" (Tune: "Frère Jacques")
  - "This Is the Way We Wave Hello" (Tune: "Here We Go 'Round the Mulberry Bush")
  - "Touch Your Toes" from *Diaper Gym*, by Priscilla Hegner and Rose Grasselli
  - "My Little Hands" from *Diaper Gym*, by Priscilla Hegner and Rose Grasselli
  - "Circle Song" (Tune: "Have You Ever Seen a Lassie?")
  - "Brown Bear, Brown Bear, What Do You See?" from *Playing Favorites*, by Greg and Steve
- Action Rhymes:
  - "Climb Aboard the Rocket Ship"
  - "Criss Cross Applesauce" from *The Kingfisher Playtime Treasury*, by Pie Corbett
- Books:
  - *Dino Shapes*, by Suse MacDonald
  - *Away We Go!*, by Chiêu Anh Urban
  - *Brown Bear, Brown Bear, What Do You See?*, by Bill Martin Jr.

Call Everyone to Storytime

Use a rain stick or other simple instrument to gather everyone's attention, saying something like "Do you hear that? It's the sound of storytime. Time for storytime!" Once everyone is settled in place, introduce yourself and welcome everyone.

Give Opening 6 by 6 Message to Caregivers

It may be a little too early to start teaching your baby the alphabet, but we can lay the groundwork for alphabet knowledge by talking about shapes. You probably play with shape-based toys at home, and we have a lot of books about shapes here at the library. Shapes are the building blocks of letters, so when we talk about circles, squares, and triangles, we're actually beginning the process of learning letters.

Sing the Welcome Song

"Peek-a-Boo" (Tune: "Frère Jacques")

Peek a boo! Peek a boo!
I see you! I see you!

I'm so glad to see you! I'm so glad to see you!
Peek a boo! Peek a boo!

Sing the Opening Song

"This Is the Way We Wave Hello" (Tune: "Here We Go 'Round the Mulberry Bush")

This is the way we wave hello,
Wave hello, wave hello.
This is the way we wave hello
So early in the morning!

Repeat with other actions such as clap our hands, touch our nose, tap our feet. Finish with wave hello once again.

Introduce and Read the Book

Away We Go!, by Chiêu Anh Urban
Point out title, author, and illustrator.

Deliver 6 by 6 Message to Caregivers

There are three reasons we read that book in today's storytime. First of all, of course, are the shapes and their relationship to letters. Second, decades of research has shown that babies naturally focus their attention on patterns of high contrasting colors. And third, when you read this book at home, your baby can reach out and actually feel the shapes that have been die-cut into the pages, allowing them to experience the book in a different way with different senses.

Lead the Action Rhyme

"Climb Aboard the Rocket Ship." Begin with baby on lap, facing caregiver.

Climb aboard the rocket ship (rock baby side to side)
We're going to the moon!
Put on your helmet (hand on baby's head)
Buckle up tight (hug baby)
We're blasting off soon!
5 . . . 4 . . . 3 . . . 2 . . . 1 . . . (bounce baby gently)
Blastoff! (raise baby high in the air)

Introduce and Play the Song

"Touch Your Toes" from *Diaper Gym*, by Priscilla Hegner and Rose Grasselli

Introduce and Play the Song

"My Little Hands" from *Diaper Gym*, by Priscilla Hegner and Rose Grasselli

Introduce and Read the Book

Dino Shapes, by Suse MacDonald

Deliver 6 by 6 Message to Caregivers

The idea that this specific dinosaur is a brachiosaur isn't important. It *is* important, however, to know that most babies start recognizing shapes and colors around five months of age. Those concepts won't necessarily have meaning for a few more months, but familiarity with shapes will eventually help them identify and categorize objects in their environment, including alphabet letters.

Introduce and Sing the Song

"Circle Song" (Tune: "Have You Ever Seen a Lassie?"). Begin with baby on lap, facing away from caregiver.

> Have you ever seen a circle, a circle, a circle (take baby's hands and make rolling movement)
> Have you ever seen a circle which goes 'round and 'round?
> It goes this way and that way, and that way and this way (rock baby side to side)
> Have you ever seen a circle which goes 'round and 'round? (make rolling movement again)

Deliver 6 by 6 Message to All Participants

We are nearing the end of our storytime, so it's time for our final story and rhyme. As you read books with your baby, or even while you're doing other activities together, notice the shapes they may be seeing and talk about them. You might be surprised how many shapes you see every day!

Introduce the Book and Song

Brown Bear, Brown Bear, What Do You See?, by Bill Martin Jr. and "Brown Bear, Brown Bear, What Do You See?" from *Playing Favorites*, by Greg and Steve

This book is great to read aloud but can also be sung to a tune similar to "Baa Baa Black Sheep." We will listen to the song while I turn the pages.

Lead the Action Rhyme

"Criss Cross Applesauce." Begin with baby on lap, facing away from caregiver.

Criss cross applesauce (use finger to make X on baby's back)
Spiders crawling up your spine (crawl fingers up baby's spine)
Cool breeze (blow on baby's neck)
Tight squeeze (hug baby)
Makes you get the sillies! (tickle baby)

Invite Participants to Extend Storytime

Invite them to stay and explore your library's children's area.

Look for Letters Everywhere: A Storytime for Talkers

This plan is appropriate for children approximately 18 months to three years old with their caregivers.

Materials you will need for this storytime:

- Music and Songs:
  - Rain stick or other simple instrument
  - "The More We Get Together" (sing or find a recorded version, such as Laurie Berkner's on the album *Buzz Buzz*.)
  - "The Freeze," by Greg and Steve from the album *Kids in Motion*
  - "Storytime Is Over" (Tune: "If You're Happy and You Know It")
- Poem:
  - "Dump Truck" from *Digger, Dozer, Dumper*, by Hope Vestergaard
- Movement Activity:
  - Scarves or ribbons to each child to use, plus ideas about making shapes in the air, such as "Can you make a small square in front of you?" and "Can you make a circle above your head?"
- Books:
  - *Digger, Dozer, Dumper*, by Hope Vestergaard

- ○ *Chicka Chicka Boom Boom*, by Bill Martin Jr. and John Archambault
- ○ *One Big Building: A Counting Book about Construction*, by Michael Dahl
- ○ *I Spy on the Farm*, by Edward Gibbs
- ○ Assorted alphabet books to display, available for checkout.

Call Everyone to Storytime

Use a rain stick or other simple instrument to gather everyone's attention, saying something like "Do you hear that? It's the sound of storytime. Time for storytime!" Once everyone is settled in place, introduce yourself and welcome everyone.

Give Opening 6 by 6 Message to Caregivers

Today's early literacy skill is **Look for Letters Everywhere.** Knowing the names and sounds of letters is a skill children need to have to be ready to learn to read. But even before they know the names of letters, they need know the names of shapes, which are the building blocks of letters. And even before that, children need to learn the concept of "same" versus "different." Most toddlers are in the stage where they are still exploring this concept and learning the names of shapes, so that's what we'll do today.

Sing or Play the Welcome Song

"The More We Get Together," traditional.

Note: Many adults are familiar with this song. If you use Laurie Berkner's recording and are not going to post all of the lyrics, be sure to make a poster with the names that Laurie sings in her version, so adults can continue to sing along.

Read/Recite the Poem

"Dump Truck" from *Digger, Dozer, Dumper*, by Hope Vestergaard

Show the picture and say there will be some dump trucks in one of today's books.

Introduce the Book

Chicka Chicka Boom Boom, by Bill Martin Jr. and John Archambault

Point out title, author, and illustrator.

Deliver 6 by 6 Message to All Participants

Our first book has lots of colorful letters in it. While I read, watch how the letters look different when they are sideways and upside down.

Read the Book

While reading, occasionally point to some of the letters as you say their names. When appropriate, pause to briefly discuss concepts or words that may be unfamiliar to toddlers.

Transition to the Next Activity

So that was *Chicka Chicka Boom Boom*, our book about tree-climbing letters. Next, let's do a song called "The Freeze"—what does "freeze" mean? If you're moving and someone says, "freeze," it means "stop." So let's dance until we hear the word "freeze," and then we'll stop.

Introduce and Play the Song

"The Freeze," by Greg and Steve
    Encourage everyone to dance and freeze along.

Transition to the Next Book

Great job! Adults, children learn with their whole bodies, and the movement and stopping is a way to explore the idea of "same" versus "different." Everyone, next we have a book about numbers—and about constructing a building. Could it be the book with the dump trucks in it? Let's see!

Introduce the Book

One Big Building: A Counting Book about Construction, by Michael Dahl

Deliver 6 by 6 Message to Caregivers

Grown-ups, there is a lot in this book that you could explore at home. Each page has its number represented in various ways, and there are hidden numbers. This is a good book for storytime, but a great book for smaller groups, too.

Deliver 6 by 6 Message to All Participants

Everybody, we're going to count a lot in this book. I hope you'll help me. (When reading, pause to count the appropriate things on each page, such as three dump trucks, seven workers, and the like.)

Read the Book

Encourage everyone to participate in counting at the right times.

While reading, pause to briefly discuss concepts or words that may be unfamiliar to toddlers.

Review the Book

I see lots of shapes in the book—look, here is a circle, and a square and some triangles . . . (Point out a few of the shapes you can see on one or two pages.)

Transition to the Next Activity

Since that book has lots of shapes, it makes me want to use our scarves (ribbons) to make some shapes in the air. Everyone, come up and get a scarf (ribbon).

Lead the Movement Activity

Direct children to make various shapes in places around their bodies. Say things like "Can you make a small square in front of you?" and "Can you make a circle above your head?" Use a scarf (or ribbon) to demonstrate, and ask adults to help children by guiding their hands if necessary. Do about five to seven different variations depending on the interest and energy of the group.

Transition to the Next Book

Great job! Adults, this was a whole-body way for children play with making shapes. Maybe later today or this week you can sit down with paper and crayons to draw shapes on paper. Everyone, our next book is about seeing many different farm animals.

Introduce the Book

I Spy on the Farm, by Edward Gibbs
    Point out title, author, and illustrator.

Deliver 6 by 6 Message to All Participants

Do you know what "I spy" means? It means "I see," and in this book we're going to see a lot of different animals. Get ready to look and guess what they are.

Read the Book

While reading, point to the letter clue and make its sound. For example, the first spread, say something like, "I spy with my little eye . . . something yellow that begins with a D. See the D right there? D sounds like /d/. What is something yellow that says 'quack, quack!' and starts with /d/, /d/, /d/?"

    Also pause to briefly discuss concepts or words that may be unfamiliar to toddlers.

Transition to the Closing Song

So that was our third book, *I Spy on the Farm*, by Edward Gibbs. Can you remember all three books we read today? (Go over the titles again, in order.) Our third book was our last book for today.

    Before we sing the closing song, I want to let everyone know that there are lots of alphabet books on display and available for checkout. ABC books are a great way to look for letters, of course, but since many of them don't have a story line, they're also good for looking at and talking about just a page at a time. Now, let's sing our goodbye song, and I'll see you next time!

Sing the Closing Song

"Storytime Is Over" (Tune: "If You're Happy and You Know It")

> Now storytime is over, wave goodbye.
> Now storytime is over, wave goodbye.
> Now storytime is done and I hope you had lots of fun,
> Our storytime is over, wave goodbye.

Invite Participants to Extend Storytime

Let people know they are welcome to come over to see the instrument you use for the call or see today's puppet. Invite them to stay and explore your library's children's area.

Look for Letters Everywhere: A Storytime for Pre-Readers

This plan is appropriate for children approximately three to five years old. Materials you will need for this storytime:

- Music and Songs:
  o "Everybody Come and Take" (Tune: "Shortnin' Bread")
  o "If You're Happy and You Know It"
  o "The Alphabet Song"
  o "Chicka Chicka Boom Boom" from *Chicka Chicka Boom Boom and Other Coconutty Songs*, by John Archambault and David Plummer
  o "Storytime Is Over" (Tune: "If You're Happy and You Know It")
- Action Rhymes:
  o "Circle Square Triangle"
  o "Where Is Red Light?" (action rhyme and flannel story)
  o "Making the Alphabet"
- Books:
  o *Perfect Square*, by Michael Hall
  o *Backseat A-B-See*, by Maria van Lieshout
  o *Chicka Chicka Boom Boom*, by Bill Martin Jr. and John Archambault

Call Everyone to Storytime

Use a rain stick or other simple instrument to gather everyone's attention, saying something like "Do you hear that? It's the sound of storytime. Time for storytime!" Once everyone is settled in place, introduce yourself and welcome everyone.

Sing the Welcome Song

"Everybody Come and Take" (Tune: "Shortnin' Bread")

> Everybody come and take
> Everybody come and take
> Everybody come and take a seat on the floor.
> Not on the ceiling,
> Not on the door,
> Everybody come and take a seat on the floor.

Sing the Opening Song

Sing a few verses of "If You're Happy and You Know It"
  Conclude with these lyrics:

Now storytime is starting sit real still,
Now storytime is starting sit real still,
Your hands are in your lap, you are sitting down real flat,
Storytime is starting sit real still.

Give Opening 6 by 6 Message to Caregivers

Today's storytime skill is **Look for Letters**, or alphabet knowledge. Before kids learn the alphabet, they need to know basic shapes. After all, shapes are the building blocks of letters! Our first story is called *Perfect Square*. In fact, if you look carefully, you'll notice the book itself is a square! Most books are rectangles, but this one is actually a perfect square!

Introduce and Read the Book

Perfect Square, by Michael Hall

Lead the Action Rhyme

"Circle Square Triangle" (use pointer finger to draw shapes in the air)

Draw a circle, draw a circle
Draw it in the sky.
Draw a circle, draw a circle
Make it round as pie.
Draw a square, draw a square
Four sides nice and straight.
Draw a square, draw a square
Four sides makes it great.
Triangle, triangle
Across, up, and down
Triangle, triangle
Sitting on the ground.

Play or Sing the Song

"The Alphabet Song"

Deliver 6 by 6 Message to Caregivers

Most kids will learn the alphabet in three steps. First they learn the names of the letters from singing the alphabet song. Then they start to recognize the shapes of letters and how they are same and different. And finally, they learn the sounds of the letters. That happens easily for some kids but takes time and practice for others. Luckily, it can be fun. Looking for letters in unexpected places is the point of this next book.

Introduce and Read the Book

Backseat A-B-See, by Maria van Lieshout

Lead the Action Rhyme

"Where Is Red Light?" (Tune: "Where Is Thumbkin?")
   (This can be made into a flannelboard with red, yellow, and green circles.)

> Where is red light? Where is red light?
> Here I am! Here I am!
> What is it you say, sir? What is it you say, sir?
> I say stop. I say stop.
> Where is yellow light? Where is yellow light?
> Here I am! Here I am!
> What is it you say, sir? What is is you say, sir?
> I say wait. I say wait.
> Where is green light? Where is green light?
> Here I am! Here I am!
> What is it you say, sir? What is it you say, sir?
> I say go! I say go!
> Red says stop. Yellow says wait.
> Green says go! Green says go!
> These are traffic signals. These are traffic signals.
> That we know. That we know.

Lead the Action Rhyme

"Making the Alphabet"

> Stretch up high, like a capital I
> Nod your head like an M

Wiggle your body like a wiggly S
And do it all over again!
Use one arm and one leg to make a big R
Use both arms to make a large K
Curve your whole body into a C
I could play this game all day!
Arms in the air to make a tall Y
Then make a huge circle for O
I'd try to make X, but it's very complex
And that's all the letters I know.

Deliver 6 by 6 Message to Caregivers

Learning the alphabet could be a really boring task, but playing "I Spy" games with shapes and letters can keep things interesting. We have a lot of traditional alphabet books and many shape books you can check out that help develop this skill. Knowledge of the alphabet in kindergarten can be connected to reading ability in the 10th grade. Ten full years later! Here's a classic alphabet book that a lot of you probably already know.

Introduce and Read or Play the Book

Chicka Chicka Boom Boom, by Bill Martin Jr. and John Archambault
   (Or simply turn the pages while playing the song from *Chicka Chicka Boom Boom and Other Coconutty Songs*, by John Archambault and David Plummer)

Sing the Closing Song

"Storytime Is Over" (Tune: "If You're Happy and You Know It")

Now storytime is over, wave goodbye.
Now storytime is over, wave goodbye.
Now storytime is done and I hope you had lots of fun,
Our storytime is over, wave goodbye.

Invite Participants to Extend Storytime

Invite them to stay and explore your library's children's area.

LOOK FOR LETTERS EVERYWHERE: A REPRODUCIBLE STORYTIME GUIDE FOR EARLY TALKERS

Call Everyone to Storytime

Give Opening 6 by 6 Message to Caregivers

It may be a little too early to start teaching your baby the alphabet, but we can lay the groundwork for alphabet knowledge by talking about shapes. You probably play with shape-based toys at home and we have a lot of books about shapes here at the library. Shapes are the building blocks of letters so when we talk about circles, squares, and triangles, we're actually beginning the process of learning letters.

Sing the Welcome Song
"Peek-a-Boo"

Sing the Opening Song
"This Is the Way We Wave Hello"

Introduce and Readthe Book
Away We Go!, by Chiêu Anh Urban

Deliver 6 by 6 Message to Caregivers

There are three reasons we read that book in today's storytime. First of all, of course, are the shapes and their relationship to letters. Second, decades of research has shown that babies naturally focus their attention on patterns of high contrasting colors. And third, when you read this book at home, your baby can reach out and actually feel the shapes that have been die-cut into the pages, allowing them to experience the book in a different way with different senses.

Lead the Action Rhyme
"Climb Aboard the Rocket Ship"

Introduce and Play the Song
"Touch Your Toes" from *Diaper Gym*

Introduce and Play the Song
"My Little Hands" from *Diaper Gym*

Introduce and Read the Book
Dino Shapes, by Suse MacDonald

Deliver 6 by 6 Message to Caregivers

The idea that this specific dinosaur is a brachiosaur isn't important. It *is* important, however, to know that most babies start recognizing shapes and colors around five months of age. Those concepts won't necessarily have meaning for a few more months, but familiarity with shapes will eventually help them identify and categorize objects in their environment, including alphabet letters.

Introduce and Sing the Song
"Circle Song"

Deliver 6 by 6 Message to All Participants

We are nearing the end of our storytime, so it's time for our final story and rhyme. As you read books with your baby, or even while you're doing other activities together, notice the shapes they may be seeing and talk about them. You might be surprised how many shapes you see every day!

Introduce the Book and Song
Brown Bear, Brown Bear, What Do You See?, by Bill Martin Jr. and
"Brown Bear, Brown Bear, What Do You See?" from
Playing Favorites, by Greg and Steve

Lead the Action Rhyme
"Criss Cross Applesauce"

LOOK FOR LETTERS EVERYWHERE: A REPRODUCIBLE STORYTIME GUIDE FOR TALKERS

Call Everyone to Storytime

Give Opening 6 by 6 Message to Caregivers

Today's early literacy skill is **Look for Letters Everywhere.** Knowing the names and sounds of letters is a skill children need to have to be ready to learn to read. But even before they know the names of letters, they need know the names of shapes, which are the building blocks of letters. And even before that, children need to learn the concept of "same" versus "different." Most toddlers are in the stage where they are still exploring this concept and learning the names of shapes, so that's what we'll do today.

Sing or Play the Welcome Song
"The More We Get Together," traditional.

Read/Recite the Poem
"Dump Truck" from *Digger, Dozer, Dumper*, by Hope Vestergaard

Introduce the Book
Chicka Chicka Boom Boom, by Bill Martin Jr. and John Archambault

Deliver 6 by 6 Message to All Participants

Our first book has lots of colorful letters in it. While I read, watch how the letters look different when they are sideways and upside down.

Read the Book

Introduce and Play the Song
"The Freeze," by Greg and Steve

Introduce the Book
One Big Building: A Counting Book about Construction,
by Michael Dahl

Deliver 6 by 6 Message to Caregivers

Grown-ups, there is a lot in this book that you could explore at home. Each page has its number represented in various ways, and there are hidden numbers. This is a good book for storytime, but a great book for smaller groups, too.

Deliver 6 by 6 Message to All Participants

Everybody, we're going to count a lot in this book. I hope you'll help me. (When reading, pause to count the appropriate things on each page, such as three dump trucks, seven workers, and the like.)

Read the Book

Lead the Activity

Have children make various shapes in places around their bodies using ribbon rings or scarves.

Introduce the Book

I Spy on the Farm, by Edward Gibbs

Deliver 6 by 6 Message to All Participants

Do you know what "I spy" means? It means "I see," and in this book we're going to see a lot of different animals. Get ready to look and guess what they are.

Read the Book

Sing the Closing Song

"Storytime Is Over" (Tune: "If You're Happy and You Know It")

LOOK FOR LETTERS EVERYWHERE: A REPRODUCIBLE STORYTIME GUIDE FOR PRE-READERS

Call Everyone to Storytime

Sing the Welcome Song
"Everybody Come and Take" (Tune: "Shortnin' Bread")

Sing the Opening Song
"If You're Happy and You Know It"

Give Opening 6 by 6 Message to Caregivers

Today's storytime skill is **Look for Letters**, or alphabet knowledge. Before kids learn the alphabet, they need to know basic shapes. After all, shapes are the building blocks of letters! Our first story is called *Perfect Square*. In fact, if you look carefully, you'll notice the book itself is a square! Most books are rectangles, but this one is actually a perfect square!

Introduce and Read the Book
Perfect Square, by Michael Hall

Lead the Action Rhyme
"Circle Square Triangle"

Play or Sing the Song
"The Alphabet Song"

Deliver 6 by 6 Message to Caregivers

Most kids will learn the alphabet in three steps. First they will learn the names of the letters from singing the alphabet song. Then they will start to recognize the shapes of letters and how they are same and different. And finally, they will learn the sounds of the letters. That happens easily for some kids but takes time and practice for others. Luckily, it can be fun. Looking for letters in unexpected places is the point of this next book.

Introduce and Read the Book
Backseat A-B-See, by Maria van Lieshout

Lead the Action Rhyme
"Where Is Red Light?" (Tune: "Where Is Thumbkin?")

Lead the Action Rhyme
"Making the Alphabet"

Deliver 6 by 6 Message to Caregivers

Learning the alphabet could be a really boring task, but playing "I Spy" games with shapes and letters can keep things interesting. We have a lot of traditional alphabet books and many shape books you can check out that help develop this skill. Knowledge of the alphabet in Kindergarten can be connected to reading ability in the 10th grade. Ten full years later! Here's a classic alphabet book that a lot of you probably already know.

Introduce and Read the Book
Chicka Chicka Boom Boom, by Bill Martin Jr. and John Archambault

Sing the Closing Song
"Storytime Is Over" (Tune: "If You're Happy and You Know It")

Looking Ahead

Look for Letters Everywhere is another of the early literacy skills children need to have experienced by about age six to be ready to learn to read. Children learn these six skills simultaneously, starting at birth, as we read, sing, and play with them. **Look for Letters Everywhere** means that children who are ready to learn to read are able to name the letters of the alphabet along with the sounds they make. Before they learn this, children must learn to recognize distinctions among items ("same" versus "different") and be able to name shapes (the building blocks of letters).

In our next chapter, we'll discuss another of the six skills, **Tell Stories About Everything**.

References

Baker, Keith. *LMNO Peas*. New York: Beach Lane Books, 2010.

Corbett, Pie. *The Kingfisher Playtime Treasury: A Collection of Playground Rhymes, Games, and Action Songs*. London: Kingfisher Books, 1989. Used with permission.

Dahl, Michael. *One Big Building: A Counting Book about Construction*. Minneapolis, MN: Picture Window Books, 2004.

Ehlert, Lois. *Eating the Alphabet: Fruits and Vegetables from A to Z*. San Diego: Harcourt Brace Jovanovich, 1989.

Emberley, Ed. *Go Away, Big Green Monster!*. Boston: Little, Brown, 1992.

Fleming, Denise. *Go, Shapes, Go!* New York: Beach Lane Books, 2014.

Franceschelli, Christopher. *Alphablock*. New York: Abrams Appleseed, 2013.

Garcia, Emma. *Tip Tip Dig Dig*. London: Boxer, 2007.

Gibbs, Edward. *I Spy on the Farm*. Somerville, MA: Templar Books, 2013.

Hall, Michael. *Perfect Square*. New York: Greenwillow Books, 2011.

MacDonald, Suse. *Dino Shapes*. New York: Little Simon, 2014.

Martin, Bill, and John Archambault. *Chicka Chicka Boom Boom*. New York: Simon & Schuster Books for Young Readers, 1989.

Rosenthal, Amy Krouse, and Tom Lichtenheld. *Duck! Rabbit!*. San Francisco: Chronicle Books, 2009.

Rueda, Claudia. *Huff & Puff: Can You Blow Down the Houses of the Three Little Pigs?*. New York: Abrams Appleseed, 2012.

Sierra, Judy. *The Sleepy Little Alphabet: A Bedtime Story from Alphabet Town*. New York: Alfred A. Knopf, 2009.

Stickland, Paul, and Henrietta Stickland. *Dinosaur Roar!*. New York: Dutton Children's Books, 1994.

Urban, Chiêu Anh. *Away We Go!: A Shape-and-Seek Book*. New York: Cartwheel Books, 2013.

Van Lieshout, Maria. *Backseat A-B-See*. San Francisco: Chronicle Books, 2012.

Vestergaard, Hope. *Digger, Dozer, Dumper*. Somerville, MA: Candlewick Press, 2013.

Chapter 9

Tell Stories About Everything

Tell Stories About Everything is also known as Narrative Skills in the early literacy field. Basically, it means that children understand that every story has a beginning, a middle, and an end.

Sequencing: A Key to Learning This Skill

The key idea behind this skill is *sequencing*—understanding concepts like first/then/last or beginning/middle/end or big/bigger/biggest. To master sequencing, children need to understand the concept of "same" versus "different." This allows them to evaluate items to determine which category or categories individual items fall into. Likewise, they can evaluate parts of a story to determine their correct order.

Children learn sequencing by doing three types of activities:

- Hearing, telling, and retelling stories
- Sorting items (such as toys, blocks, or buttons) by size, shape, color, or any other attribute
- Counting things they see

Sequencing and Stories

Sequencing also applies to many of our daily activities. Think about making a sandwich for lunch, or getting a baby's bottle ready. Both of these processes have a beginning, a middle, and an end. Knowing the structure of stories gives children the framework they need to understand stories when they begin to read them.

One way to help children learn this skill is to talk about things you do during the day. For example, when you're making lunch, you might say "Time for lunch. Let's get the bread out. Now we put cheese on it and cut it up. Our sandwich is ready. Let's eat!"

Another way to help children learn this skill is to retell stories. So after you read a book, read it—or tell it—again. Consider using puppets to retell the story, or act it out with the children. You might also draw the story with crayons on paper to retell it.

Children also learn this skill when they play with toys and props like action figures and puppets. When children use their imaginations to tell stories, they reinforce the ideas of first/then/last and beginning/middle/end.

Sequencing and Sorting

Children also learn sequencing by sorting materials. Thinking about how two items (say, a red block and a blue block of the same size and shape) may be the same and may be different requires children to identify various attributes of both blocks and understand how the blocks might be grouped into various categories. This skill directly relates to being able to tell the beginning of a story from its middle and from its end.

Sequencing and Counting

Children love to learn to count! Sequencing taps into their natural interest in putting items in order, whether it's the numbers one through ten or the phases of a caterpillar turning into a butterfly.

Activities That Help Children Develop This Skill

- Plan your day by talking about what you will do first, next, and last.
- Talk about activities while you are doing them.
- After reading, have children help you retell the story using first/then/last. So after reading *The Very Hungry Caterpillar*, you might say: "First, the caterpillar was very hungry. So he ate . . . what did he eat? After he ate all that food, he spun a cocoon, and when he came out he was a . . . "
- Encourage children to tell and retell stories using puppets, toys, or props.
- At naptime or bedtime, have children tell you the story of their day—first, this morning they got up, then had breakfast, then brushed their teeth, and then . . . ?
- Have children draw pictures and then ask them what is happening in the pictures. Write their words on their pictures or an accompanying sheet.
- Give children many opportunities to sort items like blocks or buttons by size, shape, and color. This helps children learn sequencing.
- Use stringing beads or other toys to create a sequence, and ask children to recreate the sequence.
- Count as often as you can—for example, the number of ducks on a page, the number of children at the park, anything! Numbers are an important way to learn sequencing.

Books That Are Very Good for Tell Stories About Everything

Note: Most high-quality picture books will illustrate more than one skill. These just happen to be some of our favorites to help children learn this skill.

The Adventures of Beekle: The Unimaginary Friend, by Dan Santat
An unnamed imaginary friend is lonely while waiting to be imagined, so he does the unimaginable—he sets out on a quest to find his perfect match in the real world. A wonderfully clear sequence of events allows your child to retell the story and pretend to be Beekle (as he is later named). Subtle differences in color divide this book into sections providing the perfect vehicle for stopping to ask open-ended questions about the adventure. Winner of the 2015 Caldecott medal.

Big Fat Hen, by Keith Baker
Baker's gorgeous illustrations bring fresh life into the nursery rhyme "One, Two, Buckle My Shoe." Nursery rhymes are a great way for children to hear the smaller sounds in words, and it seems nursery rhymes aren't as well used as they

have traditionally been. A book like this is a good reminder of how useful they can be, and useful for the **Tell Stories** skill, since the book is a great way to tell/retell a traditional rhyme.

Brown Bear, Brown Bear, What Do You See?, by Bill Martin Jr.
Kids and caregivers familiar with the book have likely already memorized the sequence of animals and people. If so, there may not be a need to even open the book at all! Sing the story or make story cards to use as props. Telling the story without actually reading the book will encourage deeper thinking about the order and help build the confidence of your audience members.

The Chicken Thief, by Béatrice Rodriguez
Oh dear! Fox has stolen Hen and run off with her. Will Bear, Rabbit, and Rooster be able to rescue Hen? And does she need to be rescued? Fox, though sly, may just have good intentions for Hen. This wordless book's hilarious illustrations are bound to spark a wealth of conversation. Be sure to take a look at the other books in this series to see whether Fox and Hen are able to live happily ever after.

Dog's Colorful Day: A Messy Story about Colors and Counting, by Emma Dodd
As Dog goes through his day, he makes messes and attracts colorful spots, and each comes with its own sound. "Splosh! A drop of pink ice cream lands on his right ear" . . . orange juice goes "splurt!". . . a bee drops yellow pollen, "swish!" Playing with these funny words helps children hear the smaller sounds of language. This fun title also presents the concepts of counting and colors. After reading, it's fun to retell the story by talking about the colors of Dog's spots and recalling how he got each one.

Duck on a Bike, by David Shannon
Much to the chagrin of his barnyard companions, a fun-loving duck takes a ride on a bicycle. Not only is there an incredibly strong narrative from beginning to end, but each double-page spread has its own mini story. Why exactly is the cat so disinterested? Why is the horse so smug? Make this story interactive by asking children to help Duck greet the animals as he rides by. Near the end, you can spend time on the page with all the animals on bikes to try to recall the order in which the animals appeared in the story.

Early Bird, by Toni Yuly
A simple sequence is revealed as the early bird wakes up and seeks out her breakfast. Read the book a few times and then encourage children to recall the order of events. Did the bird go up the path before or after she went under the spider web? Even the endpapers help reinforce the sequence—nighttime blue at the beginning and daylight yellow at the end.

Finn Throws a Fit!, by David Elliott
A little boy has an unexplained bad day. This story features a marvelous sequence of events that is fun to recall and retell in your own way. There are also gems in the illustrations that are worth noting, some of them seem to be begging for you to make up their own backstory.

Go Away, Big Green Monster!, by Ed Emberley
This classic book uses die-cut pages to make a monster's face appear and then disappear, feature by feature. Children feel empowered to tell the monster to "Go away!" one feature at time. Exploring the names of facial features builds vocabulary for young children and the die-cuts make for fun discussion of the shapes you can see in this book. This is a wonderful story for retelling by using a puppet, felt board, or pieces of paper. Be sure to take a look at Emberley's companion title, *Nighty Night, Little Green Monster*.

Good Night, Gorilla, by Peggy Rathmann
In this classic, nearly wordless picture book, a zookeeper thinks he's putting all the animals to bed, but a mischievous gorilla follows behind him, letting all the animals out. Everyone follows Zookeeper home to bed, and it's left to his surprised wife to get all the animals back to the zoo. Because it relies heavily on illustration, this book allows even very young children to retell the story, even after just one pass through.

The Great Gracie Chase, by Cynthia Rylant
A nice dog with a taste for freedom ignites a full neighborhood chase when she makes a break for it through an open gate. As with all cumulative tales, this one is exceptionally useful for retelling and recalling the sequence of events.

Henry Hikes to Fitchburg, by D. B. Johnson
Two bears agree to meet in the town of Fitchburg, but each chooses a different method of how to get there. Page one of this book diverges one story into two parallel lines, each with unique and distinctive points to discuss. While his friend was sweeping out the post office, what was Henry doing? Talk about a walking journey you could take, and put in order all the things you would see and do.

How Do You Make a Baby Smile?, by Philemon Sturges
This board book is rich with early literacy skills. Listen for the rhyming words, follow the sequence of animals, talk about what is happening, and have fun with the general silliness of making a baby smile. It provides a great opportunity to recite tickle rhymes and make silly animal noises, too!

If You Give a Mouse a Cookie, by Laura Numeroff
The ultimate "if/then" story is set into motion when a travelling mouse is given a cookie and subsequently asks for other things. Not all of Mouse's requests are logical, but they are all connected in some way. Use clues in the illustrations and your own experiences to guess what the mouse will ask for next and why. Once children are familiar with the story (and it won't take long!) have them pretend to be Mouse and act out the sequence.

I Went Walking, by Sue Williams
A child goes walking and finds six different animals, including a black cat, a brown horse, and a red cow, and what begins as a child walking alone becomes a child leading a parade of animals. The consistent sentence patterns make this book

a satisfying—and predictable—story for very young readers. Pointing out how the animal parade builds (first the cat, then the horse, then the cow falls in line) will help children understand the idea of beginning/middle/end in this story. The descriptions of animals—"yellow dog" and "pink pig"—builds young children's vocabulary skills.

The Lion & the Mouse, by Jerry Pinkney

An award-winning wordless retelling of the Aesop's fable. With no words, the story line is all up to you and your child. What do you see? What does it mean? What would the characters say if there *were* words on the page?

Meeow and the Little Chairs, by Sebastien Braun

Meeow, a black cat, has his friends Baa, Moo, Quack, and Woof over to play. They line up different colors of chairs; Meeow rings a bell, and Moo blows his whistle. "What can they be doing? Ding-ding! Choo-choo!" They have made a train. The simple story line and bold illustrations make this a good choice for baby and toddler storytimes. Learning the concept of colors makes this a good book for **Talk Talk Talk**. Exploring the sounds like "ding" and "choo" will help young children learn and express the **Take Time to Rhyme** skill. After reading, act out the story using chairs or pillows to reinforce the **Tell Stories** skill for children.

My Friend Rabbit, by Eric Rohmann

A loyal mouse has no other options than to trust his mischievous friend, Rabbit. The story begins and ends in the same way, but it's the wordless sequence in the middle that makes this a stellar example for this skill. Talk about the order of the animals, use the wordless pages to make up your own story, look at the emotions on the animals' faces, and give them dialogue.

The Napping House, by Audrey Wood

A classic cumulative tale in which nearly everyone is asleep . . . for a while at least. An abundance of rich words are placed carefully in this story: dozing, snoozing, dreaming, slumbering. The structure lets you hear those words over and over as you read. Try using some of these rare words in the daily conversations with children. This is a great title to have children read along with you, prompting them to repeat the phrase, "where everyone is sleeping." And because of the sharp contrast of the weather at the beginning and the end of this book, it's a great one to retell using three two-page spreads, one each from the beginning, middle, and end.

Stuck in the Mud, by Jane Clarke

"'Help! Help!' clucked the hen. 'My poor little chick! He's stuck in the mud . . . and the mud's deep and thick!'" With this panicked start, Hen enlists the help of barnyard neighbors to free her wayward son. A repeated phrase, "pushed and pulled again and again," lets young readers help tell the story, and all of that pushing and pulling makes this a fun story to retell by acting it out. Great rhymes and rhythms make this a good book for **Take Time to Rhyme**, as well. The use of expressive fonts (for instance, the letters in "pushed" are close together, and those in "pulled" are far apart) makes this a good one to use to talk about **Notice Print**.

Tell Me the Day Backwards, by Albert Lamb
A baby bear and his mother play a bedtime game recalling what they did all day starting with climbing into bed and working backwards to waking up that morning. An excellent example of how everything has a beginning, middle, and end. Try doing this with your child, maybe on a smaller scale to start and then work up to an entire day's events. It's sometimes more difficult to remember what happened before as opposed to what came next!

Tip Tip Dig Dig, by Emma Garcia
Many different types of machines work together to clean up a messy vacant lot in this interactive picture book. Preschoolers of all ages will be delighted with the surprise ending, which shows the result of all that work. This is a wonderful book for beginning/middle/end because it's easy to retell the story using three two-page spreads to illustrate the process of transforming an empty lot into something much more beautiful and useful. Be sure to invite children to make the actions of the machines while you read. You might also point out the large size of the action words (lift, tip, etc.) to help children develop the **Notice Print** skill.

The Very Hungry Caterpillar, by Eric Carle
In Eric Carle's classic tale, a too-hungry caterpillar eats too many kinds of food and ends up with a stomachache. But true to form, he ends up a butterfly, too. This story, in which an egg becomes a caterpillar, and the caterpillar becomes a butterfly, is a wonderful way to explore the idea of first/then/last with children. It also teaches sequencing through its use of counting and the days of the week.

Very Short Fairy Tales to Read Together, by Mary Ann Hoberman
Hoberman tells familiar stories like "The Three Bears" and "The Princess and the Pea" by using short poems. Color-coded words designate lines for reader one and reader two, and the simple language makes this book good to read along with children who are beginning readers. **Talkers** and **Pre-Readers** will enjoy hearing stories they know told in a different format. If you like this one, there are plenty more in the "You Read to Me, I'll Read to You" series.

Where's Spot?, by Eric Hill
Hill's innovative lift-the-flap book features Sally, a mother dog looking for her pup, Spot, in various places throughout the house. Even very young children will love interacting with this book, lifting the flaps to help Sally search for Spot. Is he inside the clock? Behind the door? This is a great one for helping young children understand beginning/middle/end—at first, Sally wonders where Spot could be; in the middle of the story, she searches for him; and at the end, she finds him.

See the last few pages of this chapter for storytime plans for babies, toddlers, and preschoolers that use some of these books.

Connecting the Skills

It's easy to see how **Tell Stories About Everything** relates to two other comprehension skills—**Have Fun With Books** and **Talk Talk Talk**. For many readers—young and old alike—it's the love of the story that brings so much pleasure to reading. As **Pre-Readers** enjoy the same story again and again, their confidence increases, and they develop a sense of pride in their knowledge of the story, its characters, plot, and nuance. This confidence can give them the courage to seek out new stories, which is the very essence of **Have Fun With Books**.

There is no better source than printed stories to provide children with a rich, deep vocabulary. Authors of picture books and easy readers judiciously choose words that deliver the most impact in a small amount of print. As a result, rare and interesting words abound in printed stories. When a new word is encountered, and a child connects it to his or her own life, that word becomes part of a vocabulary that enriches his or her own stories.

Wordless books provide a unique opportunity to combine **Tell Stories About Everything** and **Talk Talk Talk**. Just as the story differs each time you read a wordless book, so can the vocabulary. This allows children to practice new words in a comfortable story context, and adults to introduce less familiar words throughout.

Links to Lifelong Learning

People have shared stories for thousands of years. As a time-tested medium, stories have a way of teaching, entertaining, engaging, and involving storytellers and listeners alike. Reading and telling stories with young children gives them an opportunity to practice several physical and cognitive skills, including executive function (sitting still), motor skills (for participatory stories) and as mentioned earlier, sequencing. Sequencing is directly related to reading comprehension—an ability required for academic and professional success. Furthermore, being familiar with story structure may help develop oral communication skills, improving a child's ability to synthesize and verbalize thoughts in a logical way.

Storytime Plans for Tell Stories About Everything

The following section includes storytime plans for three age groups:

- **Early Talkers** (birth to approximately 18 months)
- **Talkers** (approximately 18 months to three years)
- **Pre-Readers** (approximately ages three to five years)

Feel free to adapt these plans to make them your own!

Tell Stories About Everything: A Storytime for Early Talkers

This plan is appropriate for children birth to 18 months old with a caregiver. Materials you will need for this storytime:

- Music and Songs:
    - "Peek-a-Boo" (Tune: "Frère Jacques")
    - "This Is the Way We Wave Hello" (Tune: "Here We Go 'Round the Mulberry Bush")
    - "Touch Your Toes" from *Diaper Gym*, by Priscilla Hegner and Rose Grasselli
    - "My Little Hands" from *Diaper Gym*, by Priscilla Hegner and Rose Grasselli
    - "If You're Happy and You Know It"
    - "Brown Bear, Brown Bear, What Do You See?" from *Playing Favorites*, by Greg and Steve
- Action Rhymes:
    - "Two Little Blackbirds"
    - "Criss Cross Applesauce" from *The Kingfisher Playtime Treasury*, by Pie Corbett
- Books:
    - *Early Bird*, by Toni Yuly
    - *How Do You Make a Baby Smile?*, by Philemon Sturges
    - *Brown Bear, Brown Bear, What Do You See?*, by Bill Martin Jr.

Call Everyone to Storytime

Use a rain stick or other simple instrument to gather everyone's attention, saying something like "Do you hear that? It's the sound of storytime. Time for storytime!" Once everyone is settled in place, introduce yourself and welcome everyone.

Give Opening 6 by 6 Message to Caregivers

It's true that some books have a better story line than others, but almost every book has some sort of sequence on which you can focus. For babies, look for books that have either a simple story with a sequence of events or a pattern that is repeated so you can identify and point out the book's beginning, middle, and end.

Sing the Welcome Song

"Peek-a-Boo" (Tune: "Frère Jacques")

> Peek a boo! Peek a boo!
> I see you! I see you!

I'm so glad to see you! I'm so glad to see you!
Peek a boo! Peek a boo!

Sing the Opening Song

"This Is the Way We Wave Hello" (Tune: "Here We Go 'Round the Mulberry Bush")

> This is the way we wave hello,
> Wave hello, wave hello.
> This is the way we wave hello
> So early in the morning!

Repeat with other actions such as clap our hands, touch our nose, tap our feet. Finish with wave hello once again.

Introduce the Book

Early Bird, by Toni Yuly

Deliver 6 by 6 Message to Caregivers

That book works well for **Early Talkers** because of the relatively simply illustrations and the limited text. If you have an older child, you can start talking about the parts of speech—around, through, over, and so on. However, with any age group, you can reinforce the route—or order—the bird took to get to the garden. Also notice the endpapers of the book (the pages inside the front and back covers). In the front, when the story starts, the endpapers are nighttime blue but in the back, where the story ends, they are daylight yellow!

Lead the Action Rhyme

"Two Little Blackbirds." Demonstrate actions for caregivers, though they may not be able to perform the actions if they are holding their child.

> Two little blackbirds were sitting on a hill. (hands held in front, index finger up on both hands)
> One named Jack, (wiggle right index finger)
> One named Jill. (wiggle left index finger)
> Fly away, Jack, (move right hand behind back)
> Fly away, Jill. (move left hand behind back)
> Come back, Jack! (move left hand back to front)
> Come back, Jill! (move right hand back to front)

Introduce and Play the Song

"Touch Your Toes" from *Diaper Gym*, by Priscilla Hegner and Rose Grasselli

Introduce and Play the Song

"My Little Hands" from *Diaper Gym*, by Priscilla Hegner and Rose Grasselli

Introduce the Book

How Do You Make a Baby Smile?, by Philemon Sturges

Deliver 6 by 6 Message to Caregivers

After reading that book, you can go back and talk through the order in which the animals appeared. Was the raccoon before or after the crocodile? Who was after the robin? In fact, if you check out this book to take home, you don't even have to read the words. You can tell your own story about what the animals are doing, and notice other things in the pictures that your child might recognize.

Introduce and Sing the Song

"If You're Happy and You Know It"

Deliver 6 by 6 Message to All Participants

We are nearing the end of our storytime, so it's time for our final story and rhyme. Starting right from birth, babies are busy learning about language by absorbing all of the sounds they hear. Describe what you are doing when you play together or do chores. Be sure to ask questions too, even though your baby will only be able to babble a response. That back-and-forth "conversation" will help your baby learn that words and sounds are used to communicate.

Introduce the Book and Song

Brown Bear, Brown Bear, What Do You See?, by Bill Martin Jr. and "Brown Bear, Brown Bear, What Do You See?" from *Playing Favorites*, by Greg and Steve

This book is great to read aloud but can also be sung to a tune similar to "Baa Baa Black Sheep." We will listen to the song while I turn the pages.

Lead the Action Rhyme

"Criss Cross Applesauce." Begin with baby on lap, facing away from caregiver.

Criss cross applesauce (use finger to make X on baby's back)
Spiders crawling up your spine (crawl fingers up baby's spine)
Cool breeze (blow on baby's neck)
Tight squeeze (hug baby)
Makes you get the sillies! (tickle baby)

Invite Participants to Extend Storytime

Invite them to stay and explore your library's children's area.

Tell Stories About Everything: A Storytime for Talkers

This plan is appropriate for children approximately 18 months to three years old with their caregivers.

Materials you will need for this storytime:

- Music and Songs:
  - Rain stick or other simple instrument
  - "The More We Get Together" (sing or find a recorded version, such as Laurie Berkner's on the album *Buzz Buzz.*)
  - "Storytime Is Over" (Tune: "If You're Happy and You Know It")
- Puppets:
  - Pig
  - Big Green Monster (or make a flannelboard set)
- Poem:
  - "Sit Like a Cat"
- Action Rhyme:
  - "Two Little Blackbirds"
- Books:
  - *Duck on a Bike*, by David Shannon
  - *Tip Tip Dig Dig*, by Emma Garcia
  - *Go Away, Big Green Monster!*, by Ed Emberley

Call Everyone to Storytime

Use a rain stick or other simple instrument to gather everyone's attention, saying something like "Do you hear that? It's the sound of storytime. Time for storytime!" Once everyone is settled in place, introduce yourself and welcome everyone.

Give Opening 6 by 6 Message to Caregivers

Today's skill is **Tell Stories About Everything**. This skill is important because before children learn to read, they need to understand that stories have a beginning, a middle, and an end. Retelling stories helps reinforce this idea.

Sing or Play the Welcome Song

"The More We Get Together," traditional.

Note: Many adults are familiar with this song. If you use Laurie Berkner's recording and are not going to post all of the lyrics, be sure to make a poster with the names that Laurie sings in her version, so adults can continue to sing along.

Introduce the Puppet

Show the pig puppet and say that pigs can also be called hogs. Talk about the sound hogs make, and have the children practice making the sound a few times.

Read/Recite the Poem

"Sit Like a Cat"

> Can you sit like a cat?
> Can you snort like a hog?
> Can you walk like a duck?
> Can you run like a dog?
> Can you fly like a bird?
> Can you swim like a fish?
> Can you sit still as can be?
> As still as this?

Introduce the Book

Duck on a Bike, by David Shannon
    Point out title, author, and illustrator.

Deliver 6 by 6 Message to Caregivers

An important part of the **Tell Stories** skill is learning to recognize that stories have a beginning/middle/end.

Deliver 6 by 6 Message to All Participants

In this story, Duck will say hello to a lot of animals. Can you help me read this book? We'll all say hello when Duck does. (Practice waving and saying hello. Lifting your hand to wave will give the toddlers prompts for saying hello at appropriate times throughout the book.)

Read the Book

Encourage everyone to participate in waving and saying hello.

While reading, pause to briefly discuss concepts or words that may be unfamiliar to toddlers.

Review the Book

Go back and point out the beginning/middle/end of story, using the first image of Duck on a bike, then the two-page spread of all the animals riding, then the end, when Duck puts the bike away and looks at the tractor. Ask the children what they think Duck will do next. Marking the pages with paper clips or small paper flags beforehand makes it easy to find the right images during storytime.

Transition to the Next Book

So that was our first book, the one with the duck in it. Next, we'll read a book about construction machines.

Introduce the Book

Tip Tip Dig Dig, by Emma Garcia

Deliver 6 by 6 Message to Caregivers

After reading this book, I'll show the beginning/middle/end of this story, too. Repeated activities are good for developing brains.

Deliver 6 by 6 Message to All Participants

In this story, many machines will perform many types of work. Can you help me read this book? Help me do the actions of all the machines. (Turn to two-page spread that summarizes the machines' work. Practice lifting, tipping, and so on.)

Read the Book

Encourage everyone to participate in making the machine motions.

While reading, pause to briefly discuss concepts or words that may be unfamiliar to toddlers.

Review the Book

Go back and point out the beginning/middle/end of story, using the image of the mess, then the two-page spread that summarizes the machines' work, and finally the image of the adventure playground. If you wish, mark the pages with paper clips or small paper flags beforehand.

Point out one or both of the pairs of blackbirds in the book's final spread and say, "We're going to do a rhyme about two little blackbirds and about some of the machines we saw in *Tip Tip Dig Dig*."

Lead the Group in the Action Rhyme

"Two Little Blackbirds," traditional, with additional verses by Anna Foote

> Two little blackbirds sitting on a hill
> One named Jack; the other named Jill
> Fly away, Jack! Fly away, Jill!
> Come back, Jack! Come back, Jill!
> Continue with two to three of the verses below:
> Two little diggers sitting on a hill
> One named Dig; the other named Er
> Dig away, Dig! Dig away, Er!
> Come back, Dig! Come back, Er!
> Two little dump trucks sitting on a hill
> One named Dump; the other named Truck
> Dump away, Dump! Dump away, Truck!
> Come back, Dump! Come back, Truck!
> Two little bull dozers sitting on a hill
> One named Bull; the other named Dozer
> Push away, Bull! Push away, Dozer!
> Come back, Bull! Come back, Dozer!
> Two little mixers sitting on a hill
> One named Mix; the other named Er
> Mix away, Mix! Mix away, Er!

Come back, Mix! Come back, Er!
Two little cranes sitting on a hill
One named Cr; the other named Ane
Lift away, Cr! Lift away, Ane!
Come back, Cr! Come back, Ane!
Two little road rollers sitting on a hill
One named Road; the other named Roller
Roll away, Road! Roll away, Roller!
Come back, Road! Come back, Roller!
Repeat selected verses two to three times.

Transition to the Next Book

So that was our second book, about building an adventure playground. Next, we'll read a book about a monster. But don't worry—it's a fun monster, not scary at all.

Introduce the Book

Go Away, Big Green Monster!, by Ed Emberley
    Point out title, author, and illustrator.

Deliver 6 by 6 Message to All Participants

In this story, we will tell the monster to go away. Will you help me read this book? Help me tell the monster to go away. (Practice shaking a forefinger and saying "Go away!" Lifting your forefinger will give the toddlers prompts for saying "Go away!" at appropriate times during the reading.)

Read the Book

Pause when you read off each of the monster's facial features, and ask children to point out the features on their own faces. Encourage caregivers to help children with this. Remind everyone to participate in making the monster go away. While reading, pause to briefly discuss concepts or words that may be unfamiliar to toddlers.

Review the Book

Tell the group that you will use a puppet to tell this story again, and that you will need their help.

Deliver 6 by 6 Message to Caregivers

Using the puppet to retell the story allows children to tell the story with me. At home, you could retell the story using pieces of colored paper or a whiteboard and markers. Using everyday items can help children remember and retell stories.

Retell the Story Using a Puppet

Big Green Monster, available for purchase online. There are also flannelboard patterns online, if you'd rather make your own.

Transition to the Closing Song

That was our third book, *Go Away, Big Green Monster!* Can you remember all three books we read today? (Go over the titles again, in order.) Our third book was our last book for today. So we'll sing our goodbye song, and I'll see you next time!

Sing the Closing Song

"Storytime Is Over" (Tune: "If You're Happy and You Know It")

> Now storytime is over, wave goodbye.
> Now storytime is over, wave goodbye.
> Now storytime is done and I hope you had lots of fun,
> Our storytime is over, wave goodbye.

Invite Participants to Extend Storytime

Let people know they are welcome to come over to see the instrument you use for the call, or to see today's puppet. Invite them to stay and explore your library's children's area.

Tell Stories About Everything: A Storytime for Pre-Readers

This plan is appropriate for children approximately three to five years old.
   Materials you will need for this storytime:

- Music and Songs:
  - "Everybody Come and Take" (Tune: "Shortnin' Bread")

- o   "If You're Happy and You Know It"
- o   "I Know an Old Lady Who Swallowed a Fly"
- o   "Storytime Is Over" (Tune: "If You're Happy and You Know It")
- Action Rhymes:
  - o   "Hop Like a Rabbit"
  - o   "Open Them, Shut Them"
- Books:
  - o   *My Friend Rabbit,* by Eric Rohmann
  - o   *Finn Throws a Fit!,* by David Elliott
  - o   *Tell Me the Day Backwards,* by Albert Lamb

Call Everyone to Storytime

Use a rain stick or other simple instrument to gather everyone's attention, saying something like "Do you hear that? It's the sound of storytime. Time for storytime!" Once everyone is settled in place, introduce yourself and welcome everyone.

Sing the Welcome Song

"Everybody Come and Take" (Tune: "Shortnin' Bread")

> Everybody come and take
> Everybody come and take
> Everybody come and take a seat on the floor.
> Not on the ceiling,
> Not on the door,
> Everybody come and take a seat on the floor.

Sing the Opening Song

Sing a few verses of "If You're Happy and You Know It"
  Conclude with these lyrics:

> Now storytime is starting sit real still,
> Now storytime is starting sit real still,
> Your hands are in your lap, you are sitting down real flat,
> Storytime is starting sit real still.

Give Opening 6 by 6 Message to Caregivers

Most books we use for storytime have a strong narrative. The plot starts at the beginning, some things happen in the middle, and there is generally a resolution or cliffhanger at the end. Recognizing that beginning/middle/end sequence is the heart of today's skill, **Tell Stories About Everything**. The stories we'll read today are good examples.

Introduce and Read the Book

My *Friend Rabbit*, by Eric Rohmann

Discuss the Book

Ask questions like "What animal was on the bottom of the pile? The first animal Rabbit went to get? (Elephant.) Why do you think Rabbit put the elephant on the bottom of the pile? Do you remember which animal came after elephant? (Rhino.) Does anyone remember the animal that was right underneath Rabbit before they all fell down? (Squirrel.)"

Lead the Action Rhyme

"Hop Like a Rabbit" (suit actions to words)

> Hop like a rabbit,
> Jump like a frog.
> Walk like a duck,
> Run like a dog.
> Fly like a bird,
> Swim like a fish.
> Turn around,
> And sit like this.

Introduce and Read the Book

Finn Throws a Fit!, by David Elliott

Deliver 6 by 6 Message to Caregivers

The ability to recall events, whether a sequence from a story or a retelling of the day's activity, is a precursor to reading comprehension. Reading comprehension is critical to academic success. With book like *Finn Throws a Fit!*, it's easy to go back and talk about the sequence of events—was the avalanche before or after the flood? You can even act out the story—in a safe manner!—to reinforce the sequence. There are other stories and songs that reinforce a sequence by repeating a phrase and building on it each time.

Sing or Play the Song

"I Know an Old Lady Who Swallowed a Fly"

Lead the Action Rhyme

"Open Them, Shut Them"

> Open them (hands open, palms out)
> Shut them (hands clenched into fists)
> Open them
> Shut them
> Give a little clap (clap once)
> Open them
> Shut them
> Open them
> Shut them
> Put them in your lap. (Fold hands and put in lap.)

Introduce and Read the Book

Tell Me the Day Backwards, by Albert Lamb

Sing the Closing Song

"Storytime Is Over" (Tune: "If You're Happy and You Know It")

> Now storytime is over, wave goodbye.
> Now storytime is over, wave goodbye.
> Now storytime is done and I hope you had lots of fun
> Our storytime is over, wave goodbye.

Invite Participants to Extend Storytime

Invite them to stay and explore your library's children's area.

TELL STORIES ABOUT EVERYTHING: A REPRODUCIBLE STORYTIME FOR GUIDE EARLY TALKERS

Call Everyone to Storytime

Give Opening 6 by 6 Message to Caregivers

It's true that some books have a better story line than others, but almost every book has some sort of sequence on which you can focus. For babies, look for books that have either a simple story with a sequence of events or a pattern that is repeated so you can identify and point out the book's beginning, middle, and end.

Sing the Welcome Song
"Peek-a-Boo" (Tune: "Frère Jacques")

Sing the Opening Song
"This Is the Way We Wave Hello" (Tune: "Here We Go 'Round the Mulberry Bush")

Introduce and Read the Book
Early Bird, by Toni Yuly

Deliver 6 by 6 Message to Caregivers

That book works well for **Early Talkers** because of the relatively simply illustrations and the limited text. If you have an older child, you can start talking about the parts of speech—around, through, over, and so on. However, with any age group, you can reinforce the route—or order—the bird took to get to the garden. Also notice the endpapers of the book (the pages inside the front and back covers). In the front, when the story starts, the endpapers are nighttime blue but in the back, where the story ends, they are daylight yellow!

Lead the Action Rhyme
"Two Little Blackbirds"

Introduce and Play the Song
"Touch Your Toes" from *Diaper Gym*, by Priscilla Hegner and Rose Grasselli

Introduce and Play the Song
"My Little Hands" from *Diaper Gym*, by Priscilla Hegner and Rose Grasselli

Introduce and Read the Book
How Do You Make a Baby Smile?, by Philemon Sturges

Deliver 6 by 6 Message to Caregivers

After reading that book, you can go back and talk through the order in which the animals appeared. Was the raccoon before or after the crocodile? Who was after the robin? In fact, if you check out this book to take home, you don't even have to read the words. You can tell your own story about what the animals are doing, and notice other things in the pictures that your child might recognize.

Introduce and Sing the Song
"If You're Happy and You Know It"

Deliver 6 by 6 Message to All Participants

We are nearing the end of our storytime, so it's time for our final story and rhyme. Starting right from birth, babies are busy learning about language by absorbing all of the sounds they hear. Describe what you are doing when you play together or do chores. Be sure to ask questions too, even though your baby will only be able to babble a response. That back-and-forth "conversation" will help your baby learn that words and sounds are used to communicate.

Introduce the Book and Song
Brown Bear, Brown Bear, What Do You See?, by Bill Martin Jr.
"Brown Bear, Brown Bear, What Do You See?" song from
Playing Favorites, by Greg and Steve

Lead the Action Rhyme
"Criss Cross Applesauce"

TELL STORIES ABOUT EVERYTHING: A REPRODUCIBLE STORYTIME GUIDE FOR TALKERS

Call Everyone to Storytime

Give Opening 6 by 6 Message to Caregivers

Today's skill is **Tell Stories About Everything**. This skill is important because before children learn to read, they need to understand that stories have a beginning, a middle, and an end. Retelling stories helps reinforce this idea.

Sing or Play the Welcome Song
"The More We Get Together," traditional.

Introduce the Puppet

Read/Recite the Poem
"Sit Like a Cat"

Introduce the Book
Duck on a Bike, by David Shannon

Deliver 6 by 6 Message to Caregivers

An important part of the **Tell Stories** skill is learning to recognize that stories have a beginning/middle/end.

Deliver 6 by 6 Message to All Participants

In this story, Duck will say hello to a lot of animals. Can you help me read this book? We'll all say hello when Duck does. (Practice waving and saying hello. Lifting your hand to wave will give the toddlers prompts for saying hello at appropriate times throughout the book.)

Introduce and Read the Book
Tip Tip Dig Dig, by Emma Garcia
Point out title, author, and illustrator.

Deliver 6 by 6 Message to Caregivers

After reading this book, I'll show the beginning/middle/end of this story, too. Repeated activities are good for developing brains.

From *Six Skills by Age Six: Launching Early Literacy at the Library* by Anna Foote and Bradley Debrick. Santa Barbara, CA: Libraries Unlimited. Copyright © 2016.

Deliver 6 by 6 Message to All Participants

In this story, many machines will perform many types of work. Can you help me read this book? Help me do the actions of all the machines. (Turn to two-page spread that summarizes the machines' work. Practice lifting, tipping, and so on.)

Read the Book

Lead the Group in the Action Rhyme
"Two Little Blackbirds," traditional, with additional verses by Anna Foote

Introduce the Book
Go Away, Big Green Monster!, by Ed Emberley

Deliver 6 by 6 Message to All Participants

In this story, we will tell the monster to go away. Will you help me read this book? Help me tell the monster to go away. (Practice shaking a forefinger and saying "Go away!" Lifting your forefinger will give the toddlers prompts for saying "Go away!" at appropriate times during the reading.)

Read the Book

Deliver 6 by 6 Message to Caregivers

Using the puppet to retell the story allows children to tell the story with me. At home, you could retell the story using pieces of colored paper or a whiteboard and markers. Using everyday items can help children remember and retell stories.

Retell the Story Using a Puppet

Sing the Closing Song
"Storytime Is Over" (Tune: "If You're Happy and You Know It")

TELL STORIES ABOUT EVERYTHING:
A REPRODUCIBLE STORYTIME GUIDE
FOR PRE-READERS

Call Everyone to Storytime

Sing the Welcome Song
"Everybody Come and Take" (Tune: "Shortnin' Bread")

Sing the Opening Song
"If You're Happy and You Know It"

Give Opening 6 by 6 Message to Caregivers

Most books we use for storytime have a strong narrative. The plot starts at the beginning, some things happen in the middle, and there is generally a resolution or cliffhanger at the end. Recognizing that beginning/middle/end sequence is the heart of today's skill, **Tell Stories About Everything**. The stories we'll read today are good examples.

Introduce and Read the Book
My Friend Rabbit, by Eric Rohmann

Discuss the Book

Ask questions like "What animal was on the bottom of the pile? The first animal Rabbit went to get? (Elephant.) Why do you think Rabbit put the elephant on the bottom of the pile? Do you remember which animal came after elephant? (Rhino.) Does anyone remember the animal that was right underneath Rabbit before they all fell down? (Squirrel.)"

Lead the Action Rhyme
"Hop Like a Rabbit"

Introduce and Read the Book
Finn Throws a Fit!, by David Elliott

Deliver 6 by 6 Message to Caregivers

The ability to recall events, whether a sequence from a story or a retelling of the day's activity, is a precursor to reading comprehension. Reading comprehension is critical to academic success. With book like *Finn Throws a Fit!*, it's easy to go back and talk about the sequence of events—was the avalanche before or after the flood? You can even act out the story—in a safe manner!—to reinforce the

From *Six Skills by Age Six: Launching Early Literacy at the Library* by Anna Foote and Bradley Debrick. Santa Barbara, CA: Libraries Unlimited. Copyright © 2016.

sequence. There are other stories and songs that reinforce a sequence by repeating a phrase and building on it each time.

Sing or Play the Song
"I Know an Old Lady Who Swallowed a Fly"

Lead the Action Rhyme
"Open Them, Shut Them"

Introduce and Read the Book
Tell Me the Day Backwards, by Albert Lamb

Sing the Closing Song
"Storytime Is Over" (Tune: "If You're Happy and You Know It")

Looking Ahead

Tell Stories About Everything is one of the key skills children need to have experienced by about age six to be ready to learn to read. Though it is the final skill we address in this book, we'd like to remind you that we can foster all of these skills in children simultaneously, as we read, sing, and play with them—starting from the day they are born.

In our next chapter, we'll share our thoughts on the usefulness and satisfaction of implementing a customized early literacy initiative.

References

Baker, Keith. *Big Fat Hen*. San Diego: Harcourt Brace, 1994.

Braun, Sebastien. *Meeow and the Little Chairs*. London: Boxer Books: 2009.

Carle, Eric. *The Very Hungry Caterpillar*. New York: Philomel Books, 1987.

Clarke, Jane. *Stuck in the Mud*. New York: Walker Pub., 2008.

Corbett, Pie. *The Kingfisher Playtime Treasury: A Collection of Playground Rhymes, Games, and Action Songs*. London: Kingfisher Books, 1989. Used with permission.

Dodd, Emma. *Dog's Colorful Day: A Messy Story about Colors and Counting*. New York: Dutton Children's Books, 2001.

Elliott, David. *Finn Throws a Fit!* Somerville, MA: Candlewick Press, 2009.

Emberley, Ed. *Go Away, Big Green Monster!* Boston: Little, Brown, 1992.

Emberley, Ed. *Nighty Night Little Green Monster*. New York: LB Kids, 2013.

Garcia, Emma. *Tip Tip Dig Dig*. London: Boxer, 2007.

Hill, Eric. *Where's Spot?*. New York: Putnam, 1980.

Hoberman, Mary Ann. *Very Short Fairy Tales to Read Together: (in Which Wolves Are Tamed, Trolls Are Transformed, and Peas Are Triumphant)*. New York: Little, Brown, 2012.

Johnson, D. B. *Henry Hikes to Fitchburg*. Boston: Houghton Mifflin, 2000.

Lamb, Albert. *Tell Me the Day Backwards*. Somerville, MA: Candlewick Press, 2011.

Martin, Bill, Jr. *Brown Bear, Brown Bear, What Do You See?*. New York: H. Holt, 1992.

Numeroff, Laura. *If You Give a Mouse a Cookie*. New York: Harper & Row, 1985.

Pinkney, Jerry. *The Lion & the Mouse*. New York: Little, Brown and Books for Young Readers, 2009.

Rathmann, Peggy. *Good Night, Gorilla*. New York: Putnam, 1994.

Rodriguez, Béatrice. *The Chicken Thief*. Brooklyn, NY: Enchanted Lion Books, 2010.

Rohmann, Eric. *My Friend Rabbit*. Brookfield, CT: Roaring Brook Press, 2002.

Rylant, Cynthia. *The Great Gracie Chase*. New York: Blue Sky Press, 2001.

Santat, Dan. *The Adventures of Beekle: The Unimaginary Friend*. New York: Little, Brown, 2014.

Shannon, David. *Duck on a Bike*. New York: Blue Sky Press, 2002.

Sturges, Philemon. *How Do You Make a Baby Smile?* New York: HarperCollins, 2007.

Williams, Sue. *I Went Walking*. San Diego: Harcourt Brace Jovanovich, 1990.

Wood, Audrey. *The Napping House*. Orlando, FL: Harcourt, 2004.

Yuly, Toni. *Early Bird*. New York: Feiwel and Friends, 2014.

Conclusion

The Benefits and Usefulness of Creating a Unique Early Literacy Initiative

Launching an early literacy program like **6 by 6** is a rewarding experience. As Mary G. Boller from Northwest Kansas Library System states, "I have had parents tell me that their children had a head start to reading and learning by utilizing the six skills of **6 by 6**. As a community of educators, we sometimes believe that parents know exactly what they can do to enhance their children's chance of success, but they don't *always* know what they can do to make a difference. This program puts the tools in the hands of all who serve the needs of young children and their families."

Boller continues, "Early literacy jumpstarts a lifetime of reading and learning." Isn't that exactly what every children's librarian wants to foster in local communities?

A literacy program of your own allows you to tailor materials and approaches to best meet the needs of your community. Begin developing your program with a few core beliefs:

- Public libraries have a place in early education.
- Outreach is a key component of an early literacy initiative.
- The entire community wants what's best for children.

Public Libraries Have a Place in Early Education

Before they are old enough for preschool or kindergarten, kids are welcome in the public library. For kids who *are* enrolled in formal early education programs, the public library offers a weekend and evening place to play, explore, read, socialize, and interact.

Alongside school and home, the library strives to be the "third place" where families spend a large portion of their free time. It is clear that the public library plays a very important role in early education. Johnson County Library's former outreach librarian Kathy McLellan accentuates the library's unique place in early literacy, saying, "Early education is not universal [so] the library is early school. Families and young children go to the library to educate themselves and assimilate into culture at large."

Outreach Is a Key Component of an Early Literacy Program

The people not currently visiting their local public library are the very definition of an underserved population. If at all possible, include outreach as a cornerstone of your early literacy services. Many nonusers view the library as a cultural relic with no pertinence to their lives. It is up to you to change their minds!

As Sandra Wilkerson from Southeast Kansas Library System says, "Taking **6 by 6** to the county fair, ball fields, parks, and festivals are ways that the library can reach more people and spread the word. I always encourage librarians to take brochures to these events to get exposure. You never know who will show up when you are outside the library walls!"

An early literacy program allows you to showcase the library's vital role in your community; outreach allows you to reach patrons in ways both convenient and relevant to their lives. In other words, it refocuses public attention onto what you do best: inspire readers and provide them with resources that inform and enrich their lives.

Everyone Wants the Best for Children

Everyone wants the best for our children, and many are willing to work for their welfare. No matter how well intentioned, there are always new parents who need to be informed that brain development happens rapidly in the first five years.

McLellan states, "You are never done making people aware that it's an important thing." Melendra Sutliff Sanders of North Central Kansas Libraries System concurs, saying, "Even many highly educated parents don't really understand the impact of early literacy activities on their children's early development and future learning. By focusing on early literacy, libraries provide children with fun experiences that help them gain skills necessary to be prepared to learn in school, and libraries teach parents ways to further help their children."

Everyone in the community benefits from children having a solid early literacy foundation. Sanders says, "Talk to everyone about early literacy. This is something that interests all parents, all teachers, all grandparents, all pediatricians. And even people who aren't parents, teachers, grandparents, or pediatricians are sometimes interested. The best way to find partners in an early literacy initiative is to talk about it!"

Johnson County Library's former communications director Kasey Laine Riley concurs. She states, "The need for early childhood literacy education transcends race, class, and education level and is ever-present. Each year nearly four million children are born in the U.S. and the greater the knowledge each person in that child's life has regarding early childhood literacy, the greater the likelihood the child will be well prepared to learn in school."

You may find it helpful to make a list of talking points for different audiences. You will emphasize different aspects of early literacy to a parent than you will to a business owner, and you'll give yet another set of details to a potential funder. All of those people are important for your mission, and the more people in the community who understand your goal, the greater success you'll have creating a well-integrated and thoroughly supported program.

There is no better reason for putting forth effort to design and launch an early literacy program than setting children up for lifelong success. And it *is* an effort. In this book you've read about the route taken by Johnson County Library and the State Library of Kansas to create the successful program that Kansas library patrons enjoy today.

Your route will be impacted by your own library's mission, space and time constraints, budgetary issues, staffing, community response, and demographics. **6 by 6** has many moving parts and involves dozens of people talking about it daily with Kansas families. However, your program does not have to be as complex. Start small and expand as you gain support and momentum.

As you start, be mindful of the quality of your interactions with patrons rather than the quantity. You may be introducing the library to a brand new father who feels overwhelmed but is still committed to providing the best possible start for his daughter. You may be comforting a grandmother who hasn't set foot in a library in 30 years but is now raising her young grandson. Your storytime may be filled with English language learners who are looking to you to help them (and their children) learn the complexities of our language. No matter the situation, every contact you make could have a lasting effect on a future reader.

It's an awesome responsibility. It's a rewarding prospect. As Boller says, "If you can meet the needs of young children and families in your area you will have formed a relationship that will last for a lifetime."

References

Boller, Mary G., personal communication with the authors, March 2015.
McLellan, Kathy, in discussion with Bradley Debrick, March 2015.
Sanders, Melendra Sutliff, personal communication with the authors, March 2015.
Wilkerson, Sandra, personal communication with the authors, March 2015.

Index

About the Authors

ANNA FOOTE became the first-ever staff member focused on youth services at the State Library of Kansas when she was hired as early literacy/lifelong learning coordinator in 2012. At the State Library, Anna supported the adoption of **6 by 6: Ready to Read** by Kansas libraries of all sizes. Before joining the State Library, Anna was a youth services librarian at Johnson County Library, where she served as part of the team that developed, tested, and implemented **6 by 6** at Johnson County Library's Antioch location, which served as the creative incubator for **6 by 6**.

Anna's first library job was as a traveling "storytime lady" for the outreach department of the Kansas City (MO) Public Library. She traveled the city, story bag over her shoulder and monkey puppet in hand, visiting thousands of children in hundreds of home- and center-based child education programs.

Anna earned a BA in English from the University of Kansas and an MLIS from the University of Missouri, Columbia. She currently works at Northeast Kansas Library System, where she provides youth services and continuing education consulting services to school, academic, and public libraries throughout a 14-county region.

BRADLEY DEBRICK joined the Johnson County Library as a part-time adult information specialist in 1999 and transferred into youth services—his true passion—in early 2000. After receiving his master's degree, he served as youth services librarian at two branch locations including the Antioch branch, where he and Anna worked together during the very early days of **6 by 6**.

Bradley is now Johnson County's early literacy coordinating librarian, a position dedicated to overseeing the library's early literacy efforts. He divides his time between outreach in the community, staff training, partnerships with other child-serving agencies, and developing activities for the library's 13 in-branch early literacy activity spaces.

Bradley has a BS in elementary education from Emporia State University and an MLS from the University of North Texas.